D1603011

Undiversified

UNDIVERSIFIED

THE BIG GENDER **SHORT** IN INVESTMENT MANAGEMENT

ELLEN CARR AND KATRINA DUDLEY

Columbia Business School
Publishing

Columbia University Press
Publishers Since 1893
New York   Chichester, West Sussex
cup.columbia.edu

Library of Congress Cataloging-in-Publication Data
Names: Carr, Ellen (Portfolio manager), author. | Dudley, Katrina
(Portfolio manager), author.
Title: Undiversified : the big gender short in investment management / Ellen
Carr and Katrina Dudley.
Description: New York : Columbia University Press, [2021] | Includes index.
Identifiers: LCCN 2020052039 (print) | LCCN 2020052040 (ebook) | ISBN
9780231195881 (hardback) | ISBN 9780231551533 (ebook)
Subjects: LCSH: Investment advisors. | Portfolio managers. | Women in finance. |
Portfolio management—Social aspects. | Financial services industry—Vocational
guidance. | Sex discrimination in employment.
Classification: LCC HG4621 .C3728 2021 (print) | LCC HG4621 (ebook) | DDC
332.6082—dc23
LC record available at https://lccn.loc.gov/2020052039
LC ebook record available at https://lccn.loc.gov/2020052040

Cover design: Lisa Hamm

DISCLAIMER

This publication is distributed with the understanding that the authors are not engaged in rendering professional services, professional advice, or other expert assistance in this book. If any such services, advice, or assistance are sought by the reader, the services of a professional who can assist the reader should be sought. Neither the authors nor the publisher is liable for any actions prompted or caused by the information presented in this book. Any views expressed herein are those of the authors and do not represent the views of the organizations the authors work for.

Contents

Contents

Prologue

When you think of someone who manages money, do you think of a man or a woman?

If you answered "woman," you're unusual. You are not necessarily wrong, but the odds aren't in your favor. The headline statistics—the genesis of this book—speak for themselves: only 10 percent of portfolio managers (PMs—the people managing and investing your money) are women, and investment management (IM)[1] firms majority-owned by women manage less than 1 percent of global investable assets.[2]

Your authors are, in this respect, the 10 percent and 1 percent, respectively. We manage money in the equity and fixed-income asset classes at a large mutual fund manager and a small, majority-women-owned institutional manager. We *love* our jobs. We consider ourselves blessed to work in the investing industry—and to do so largely unscathed by the blatant sexism that gets a lot of coverage in other industries.

When we saw the statistics quoted above, we weren't exactly shocked—but it got us thinking. Why don't we work with more women? What is it about IM that has resulted in a gender imbalance that rivals that of Silicon Valley, television comedy, and other bro-culture arenas? Why is there only one of us for every nine men in the room when we attend industry conferences? We've both been in this industry for more than twenty years—and seen little change in the gender of our peers over these two decades.

As we began talking informally to peers in the industry, as well as some who have left, we came to five conclusions about IM's diversity problem. Our growing sense of puzzlement about the questions they raised led us to write this book.

1. Finance itself has a diversity problem, but it's not nearly as severe as that of IMs. GAO (Government Accounting Office) data shows that women make up a third to half of employees in financial services broadly. They are much better represented in banks and insurance companies, for example, than in IM. Why does our sliver of the finance infrastructure exclude women?

2. Diversification is Investing 101—yet we don't do it in our personnel ranks. Why does an industry that insists on adequate diversification for its clients have a blind spot where its practitioners are concerned?

3. Active investment management has failed to generate returns in excess of the market, after accounting for the fees charged to clients. The clients for whom we manage money have woken up to this and are shifting into low-fee, passive strategies that seek to match a benchmark rather than make active bets on individual holdings. Isn't it at least *possible* that the industry's failure to meet clients' expectations results from its homogeneous workforce? This is your (and our) retirement money and college savings we're talking about! Don't we owe it to ourselves and our clients to figure out why we're not generating the results we promised, and ask tough questions about the role our homogeneity might play in this failure?

4. No book about IM would be complete without a discussion of the rise of passives. We believe that this represents an opportunity for women, as competing for assets requires differentiation,

and diversity is a pillar of that. For all the disruption passives have caused, active IM still dominates the industry (and we are both beneficiaries of its tenacity); the battle for assets is still active management's to lose.

5. Money is power. Whether you lament or embrace this statement, you probably agree with it. Investment management is at the epicenter of *our* money and *your* money. Our industry pays us quite well—which means that as long as only 10 percent of us are women, the industry is contributing disproportionately to the wage gap that permeates corporate America. Why do men get to take home the lion's share of IM profits and hold the power that comes from wielding a big checkbook? And our industry is in charge of allocating your capital, which means making decisions about which companies and business models deserve your investment. Why is *your* money, and the power that goes along with investing it, in mostly male hands?

We hope that we don't have to prove this point in 2021, but we will make it nonetheless: increasing gender diversity is not a "feel good" issue in IM—it is imperative. Gender diversity isn't merely equitable or fair—it makes good business sense. Active IM is particularly ripe for a revolution in its personnel ranks. It is under siege from passive IM on the one hand and technological innovation on the other. As IM firms struggle to adapt to these twin threats, we are writing this book to ask, why *shouldn't* gender parity be part of the solution to our industry's woes?

With these questions ringing in your ears, you will read about the dearth of female PMs in three sections in this book:

1. Definition: an overview of the IM industry and the career path and role of the portfolio manager, ending with a deep dive into statistics on female representation at money management firms. The intent of this section, which we anticipate some industry

participants will skip, is to provide an understanding of the IM industry and investing careers that are available, as well as an overview of the industry's gender demographics.

2. Diagnosis: an investigation of the reasons for the male dominance of IM, drawing on the two authors' collective four decades in the industry, analysis of the undergraduate and MBA "supply chain" into investment management, interviews with successful women investors as well as those who left the industry, and the authors' own stories.

3. Solutions, from three perspectives: (a) how to address the industry's image problem at the earliest stage of recruiting (college/MBA); (b) how to keep, support, and promote women once they opt into the career; and (c) how various organizations and people are striving to change the industry's gender composition. Our "Money Manifesto," the last chapter, is a challenge to the industry to ensure that women are no longer the salient minority at IM firms but, rather, are broadly and fairly represented in this lucrative, fulfilling career.

We will say this early and often: let's not blame men for IM's gender imbalance. Instead, let's see what we can do differently to encourage more women to pursue IM careers. By all means, let's celebrate the women who have made it to the top of the IM game, who are running IM firms, beating the market and hanging out their own shingles against the odds—while acknowledging that their career paths and, in many cases, their very personalities are unusual.

A Word on Terminology

If you're new to the world of IM, we will be using some terms that might be unfamiliar in this context, or that might be slightly different from the words you associate with investing. We'll do our best to define these as we go; for now, here are two that we use throughout the book.

1. Investment management (IM). Here's the Investopedia definition: *Investment management refers to the handling of financial assets and other investments. The term most often refers to managing the holdings within an investment portfolio, and the trading of them to achieve a specific investment objective. Investment management is also known as money management, portfolio management, or wealth management.* Investment management is also known as fund management, asset management, money management, or simply investing. Throughout the book we will use these terms interchangeably.

2. Portfolio manager (PM). Here's the Investopedia definition: *A portfolio manager is an individual who develops and implements investment strategies for individuals or institutional investors.* The PM role is our primary focus in this book, as PMs are responsible for the day-to-day management of your money. Confusingly, many people in IM are called PMs, including wealth managers, financial advisors, and institutional or client PMs. Our book is about the people who focus on the analytical side of investing rather than those who focus on selling investment solutions to individual and institutional investors.

We've kept the industry jargon because we think your mastery of it will give you a leg up as you're interviewing—whether that means interviewing for a job or interviewing someone to become your financial advisor. In case it becomes overwhelming, at the end of this book we've included a glossary with the terms you're likely to encounter—here and in our industry.

Gender Diversity Versus Other Types of Diversity

This book focuses on the topic of gender diversity specifically. We hope that someone will write a book about other, equally troubling diversity gaps in IM. We have heard from non-Caucasian men that the issues women face in the industry ring true for them as well, so we believe that some of our takeaways will prove useful to male minorities.

Where Is My Female Warren Buffett?

There is no female Warren Buffett—a North Star women can aspire to emulate. The CFA Institute, the industry's primary professional network, found in diversity and inclusion workshops that 71 percent of the participants listed talent acquisition as one of the top three reasons for diversity/inclusion—that is, casting a wider net helps find great talent.[3] Yet talent acquisition is impaired by the lack of role models: Why would you want to go to work in an industry in which no one looks like you or has the life you want to have? We heard this echoed in our interviews across generations, from senior PMs to undergraduates considering the career:

Women are intimidated because there are no role models.

If the only stories that you know are of people who aren't anything like you, don't have any experience like you, don't look anything like you, don't remind you of anything about yourself . . . then you kind of think, is this really for me?

I've never had a female mentor.

Females look to other female "heroes," but they don't see other females in this job.

If anything, thanks to survivor bias, the women who make it to the top of the industry are sometimes overwhelmingly impressive. As one of our interviewees said, "While there's room for lots of different male personality types in our industry, I've observed that really only one female personality type works well in IM, and it's so high-achieving that it can be intimidating as a role model."

In interviewing dozens of successful women for our book, we did consider identifying—inaugurating—one to be the North Star for women aspiring to careers in IM. Believe us when we say that there are plenty of great candidates. But we ultimately decided that a constellation made up of different models of success—that is, "stars"—rather than a singular North Star is a more meaningful construct. Why? For one thing, exposure in our industry is of dubious value. With the exception of a few high-profile investors who sometimes come across as obnoxious, rich old white men—we won't name names here, but you know who they are—our industry is pretty anonymous, because managing big piles of money requires a dose of paranoia. If you work at one of the world's biggest fund managers, you don't want too much coverage of your investment strategies for fear that others will copy them. And let's not forget that Warren Buffett had the luxury of starting as a relatively unknown investor in a relatively unknown area of the country. There were no smartphones—and no immediate exposure or feedback when you made a big call or trade. Today there is nowhere to hide, and successful women in IM are already under intense pressure because they are a rare breed. The additional pressure of having to represent the industry's token woman, competing with the aforementioned high-profile men, offers limited upside, with plenty of downside potential. Call this a poor risk–reward investment.

And we don't want to discourage you by relating the incredible success stories of some of our interviewees; instead, we encourage you to keep the concept of survivor bias close at hand when you benchmark yourself against some of these women. When you read our constellation chapter, we hope you'll hear the message that we heard repeatedly: IM professionals (including us!) love their jobs—the continual learning, intellectual stimulation, and constantly changing investment landscape. We hope that reading about these women will inspire you to enter or continue in the field of investment management, knowing that there are lots of women—including, especially, us!—who have your back.

Let's do away with the prototypical money manager image we used to open this prologue. And let's get rid of the Ginger Rogers expectations that many of us have felt working alongside mostly men while we're at it. Many of us feel that we've had to dance in heels, backwards, to have successful IM careers.

Let's kick off our heels—it's time to move.

Undiversified

PART ONE

The Industry, the Jobs, and the Gender Imbalance

A Reading Roadmap Based On Your Background

This book is aimed at a broad audience: from an undergraduate reviewing her career options, to the seasoned portfolio manager who has spent thirty years in investing and remembers being the *only* woman in *every* room. To ensure that our content is accessible to everyone, the first two chapters provide an overview of the investment management (IM) industry and the two jobs at its heart: analyst and portfolio manager. If you have worked in the industry for more than a couple of years, you might skim or even skip these chapters. If you're new to our industry and have questions such as "what's the difference between a financial advisor and a portfolio manager?" we hope to answer them before we dig into the subject matter of the book. And if you're somewhere in between—say, an analyst at an IM firm—you might find that chapter 2 gives you some tips on making the transition from analyst to PM.

Whatever you do, don't skip chapter 3, as it introduces the problem this book is aimed at diagnosing and (if we might humbly say) solving: the dearth of women investors. Here you'll find gender data about various professional industries to show just how far behind IM is compared with law, medicine, and other knowledge-based professions. We'll also look at the limited amount of performance data available to assure you that there's no male chromosomal advantage in investing. We're not traveling in uncharted territory in any of part I; rather, we are consolidating data from our industry in one place and animating it with the voices of some of our interviewees. We hope you'll leave this section with a better understanding of the industry, the job, and the vast gender disparity at its core.

1

An Overview of the Active Investment Management Industry

Who Uses Investment Management?

YOU probably do—if you've got money saved someplace other than a bank savings account.

What are you saving for? Retirement is the most typical answer to this question—a response that has become more common in the past several decades, as responsibility for funding our retirement has shifted from corporations (via pension plans) and the government (via Social Security) to each of us.

In the theoretical good old days, you or your spouse might have worked for a large company with a pension that promised to pay you a certain amount on retirement, until your death or that of your spouse. This is called a "defined benefit," or DB, plan. Although pension plans still exist, companies have been freezing them, which typically means closing them to new employees, as they seek to cut costs and limit their liability exposure. And even if you're fortunate enough to participate in a DB plan, thanks to the magic of pension accounting rules, most pensions are underfunded—meaning there is not enough money to pay pensioners what they've been promised. In fact, of the 338 pension plans offered by companies in the S&P 500, only 18 are fully funded. These pension funds did, and still do, use sophisticated money managers to invest optimally, but they are hardly perfect. For example, until the passing of the 1974 ERISA Act, which limited the amount the pension plan could invest in the employer sponsor's own stock to 10 percent, corporate pension plans occasionally went bust because they loaded up on stock of their sponsor company. Imagine if you worked at Enron and all of your pension was invested in Enron stock—you'd be flipping burgers in your golden years. Fortunately, as ERISA took hold, pension investments became the provenance of experienced professional investors—or, as they are typically referred to in the industry, portfolio managers (PMs).

The replacement of the corporate pension plan with IRAs, 401(k)s, and the like, known as "defined contribution" (DC) plans, has transferred more decision-making—and, arguably, more risk—into the hands of people like you. During the 1980s and 1990s, paralleling the demise of the corporate pension plan, the mutual fund industry saw impressive growth. According to the Investment Company Institute (ICI), 45 percent of U.S. households own mutual funds,[1] of which there are 114,000 in existence, with $48 trillion in investments.

A mutual fund is a pooled investment vehicle that aggregates the assets of smaller, individual investors to provide the type of diversification and liquidity that used to be reserved for wealthy investors. Mutual funds provide individual investors with diversification because an investment in a mutual fund means that your money is pooled with other people's money and invested across a large number of individual stocks. They provide liquidity because mutual fund investors can generally liquidate their investments within a few days.[2]

The mutual fund industry has evolved to provide a broad range of investment options for individual and corporate investors. Whether you've got a little or a lot to invest—no matter how many zeroes you've put behind the first numeral in your quest to retire or save for a house down payment or your kids' egregiously expensive college education—you've probably put this money somewhere other than under your mattress. If in fact you've put it under your mattress, you are implicitly making the assumption that the Federal Deposit Insurance Corporation (FDIC) does not have sufficient resources to stand behind the roughly $12 trillion on deposit at U.S. banks—which is a pretty strong, arguably paranoid, statement, albeit not a completely irrational one. It's been little more than a decade since the financial crisis of 2008, when the question "Should I worry about the money in my Bank of America checking account?" was cocktail party chatter.

What you've done with the money depends on your goals for it and your risk tolerance. If you don't want to risk losing any of it, it's probably in that BofA account, or maybe a CD or short-maturity Treasury bond. But the portion you're saving for retirement is likely to be invested in more risky assets than these "full faith and credit" instruments—that is, backed by the promise of Uncle Sam and the U.S. Treasury.

If you're invested in "risk" assets, you're doing it in one of several ways.

1. You're DIY-investing, choosing the individual stocks and bonds you want in your portfolio. This is generally frowned on, not just by the investment managers of the world, who certainly have a vested interest in your unwillingness to do this, but also by most reasonable people who would liken this to putting a cast on your own broken leg rather than going to a doctor.

2. You're completely hands-off and have entrusted your money to a financial advisor. You might also refer to this person as your broker or money manager—although in the IM industry, "money manager" is generally used interchangeably with "portfolio manager" to refer to the person or people directly investing in companies and countries. In this book we use the term "portfolio manager," or PM, to describe this function. Unless you have $1 million or more to invest (the minimum level for a "qualified"—aka special—type of investor), this advisor generally selects a group of mutual funds for you rather than a group of stocks. Your Edward Jones or Merrill Lynch guy is not investing your portfolio in Apple stock; he is investing it in a mutual fund that

owns AAPL, along with a multitude of other stocks and likely another fixed-income or bond mutual fund for diversification. His primary job is to figure out the right mix of stock and bond mutual funds for you, which depends on, among other things, your risk appetite, your age, and how soon you're planning to use the money.

There is a wide range of expertise in this part of the investment management supply chain (which is not the focus of our analysis and research), ranging from people who have complex models and decades of investing experience underlying their decisions, to unethical folks who "churn" (an efficient way of saying buy and sell frequently) your money to generate commissions. Oh, yes, by the way, you're paying your advisor a commission, known in the industry as a "12b1 fee." This commission comes out of the fee charged by the mutual fund, known as a "management fee." The exact divvying up of these two types of fees between the advisor and the mutual fund company is a delicate dance.

We discuss fees and expenses in more detail later in this chapter. For now, understand that although the industry is becoming more transparent about fees, it's still difficult to calculate the fees you're being charged, and there are several ways in which your advisor and investment manager might be earning their fees. Recent industry trends suggest that investment management firms and financial advisors are changing their fee structures and moving toward a model by which advisors charge clients (i.e., you) a fixed-percentage fee based on how much of your assets they are managing.

3. You're somewhere in between these two extremes and have decided to use a low-cost brokerage account (held at, for example, Charles Schwab) to invest in a selection of mutual funds. Here you are deciding on your own asset allocation—choosing the amount of stocks and bonds you want yourself—and outsourcing the choice of the individual stocks and bonds to a mutual fund manager. You are paying the management fee set by the funds you choose but not the added layer of fees that goes to your financial advisor, and, of course, you are not receiving his expertise.

In each of these scenarios, you could be following the method with your 401(k), 403(b), or IRA, or your kids' 529 plan (tax-exempt investments), or you could be doing it with the money you've saved outside of a retirement account (taxable investments).

Active Versus Passive: What Am I Paying All These Fees For?

Once you've decided that you're going to invest in a fund—whether a mutual fund or an exchange-traded fund (ETF), which are functionally similar—you have an additional decision to make: whether you want to invest in a fund that is actively or passively managed. Active management means what it sounds like: a team of people—generally a portfolio manager, several analysts, and a trader—is responsible for investing a pool of money, including the money that you have invested and that of many other investors, who are referred to as the "shareholders" of a mutual fund. This team, not just the portfolio manager alone, does the day-to-day work of analyzing companies and deciding whether to invest in them. These are intellectually and even physically demanding jobs requiring several skills, including intensive Excel modeling, travel (to meet with the companies' management teams), reading, and writing. Don't feel sorry for active investment managers' exhausting lives—we are generally well-compensated for the intensity of our career. We will explore the jobs associated with active IM in more detail in chapter 2.

The reason you choose an active manager is because you think he will gain you higher returns in good markets and less horrible returns in bear markets. For example, in a year in which the S&P 500, a reasonable gauge of the overall U.S. stock market, goes up by 10 percent, an active manager would hope for his portfolio to go up by more than 10 percent. Perhaps more important to the typical investor, if the S&P 500 has a negative return, an active PM might reasonably be expected to keep his clients from losing as much money as the overall market by, we'd hope, avoiding the worst-performing stocks in the index.

Of course, this management isn't free—that's what the management fees referenced earlier are for. These fees are expected to cover the costs of running the fund, including the salaries of PMs, analysts, and traders; their $24k/year Bloomberg terminals; their late nights at the bar with colleagues after grilling members of the C-suite; and their airline travel and hotel stays. The fees also cover compliance, an expense that has grown substantially with increased regulation, and administrative costs such as generating shareholder reports, as well as the cost of a mutual fund board. These board members are the stewards of the money that is managed, with responsibility for hiring and, in very rare cases, firing the manager of those assets.

Unfortunately, actively managed funds by and large have failed to deliver on their promises. According to a mid-year 2019 S&P study, "Over longer-term horizons (ten to fifteen years), at least 80 percent of active managers underperformed their respective benchmarks across all domestic equity categories."[3] Or, as Howard Marks of Oaktree Capital observed ironically: "For decades active managers have charged fees as if they've earned them."[4]

Oops.

The fees you're paying the investment manager are a big part of the reason for this underperformance. In the absence of these fees, the returns of many actively managed funds roughly match the returns of the underlying index—but, of course, they have promised to do much better than that. The industry has also been a victim of its own success: with the proliferation of mutual funds, a lot of bad ones have come into existence. When the mutual fund was introduced during the Roaring Twenties, there was little competition. But today it's much more difficult to carve out a competitive advantage through superior research insight, technological models, data sorting, and so on. It's crowded out there for active investment management.

When an active manager underperforms the market, the fund generally loses assets. In the past, investors would redeem their mutual fund holdings and give them to another active investment manager.

But these days, when active managers underperform their index—which, as discussed, they tend to do—investors have a new option: passive investing strategies, also known as "indexing." An index fund has one goal: to match the performance of a given index. It's not trying to protect you from bad markets or "juice" your returns in good ones; it simply replicates the holdings, and thus the performance, of a relevant index. For example, both the S&P 500 index and the Vanguard S&P 500 Index Fund (ticker[5] VFINX) returned 22 percent in 2017. Of course, an investor in an index fund will also ride it down—both VFINX and the S&P 500 lost 37 percent of their value in 2008.

Index funds charge very low fees, a fraction of those charged by active funds. In 2018, the active to passive fee spread was 45 basis points (or bps).[6] Index funds have, rather than a team of people furiously churning out models and analyses, a few folks who make sure the fund matches whatever index it is replicating. The biggest index players are Blackrock and Vanguard, but many fund managers now offer some type of passive strategy—even if they are primarily viewed as active managers. In fact, several firms—including one of the leaders in the active IM industry, Fidelity—have rolled out zero-cost index funds. PwC estimates that passively managed strategies will account for 22 percent of global assets under management (AUM) by the end of 2020—double their 11 percent share in 2012.[7] The passive share grab has been most pronounced in U.S. stocks: passively managed U.S. stock strategies are projected to reach parity with actively managed ones by 2025.[8] The collective gasp you hear on reading that statistic is from all of us who manage money actively. This is not good for the firms we work for or for our compensation.

Passive strategies are gaining share in other asset classes, too. You can invest in the Vanguard Bond Fund (ticker BND), which attempts to replicate the performance of an investment-grade bond index like the Barclays Aggregate Bond Index, the bond market's equivalent of the S&P 500. Indexing has been slower to catch on in fixed-income/bond investing, primarily because of the more complex structure of the fixed-income markets. There are, for example, roughly 10,000 holdings in the Barclays Aggregate Bond Index, and it would be almost impossible to buy each of these securities. It is much easier to replicate the S&P 500 index, which requires only 500 holdings, all of which are exchange-traded and easy to buy and sell.

Articles such as William Sharpe's "The Arithmetic of Active Management"[9] highlight the tension between the active and passive camps: "Today's fad is index funds that track the Standard & Poor's 500. True, the average soundly beat most stock funds over the past decade. But is this an eternal truth or a transitory one?" Sharpe's article, though published in 1991, has aged well; this debate has only intensified over the ensuing decades, with no clear answer to the question he posed thirty years ago.

Given how high the stakes are for active management, it's no wonder that several anti-passive arguments exist.

- Some industry experts believe that the pendulum will swing back toward active management in the next bear market, when active managers can avoid excessive losses with portfolios that diverge sharply from the overall market or index. As we live through the 2020 pandemic panic and rally, this has yet to play out. (Granted, it's a very short and unusual time frame in which to evaluate any investment results or make bold statements about the future of active management.)
- Some take issue with the calculation of passive-strategy returns. Robeco researchers David Blitz and Milan Vidojevic, in their study, "The Performance of Exchange-Traded Funds,"[10] found that ETFs have an annualized alpha of -75bps when evaluated the same way as mutual funds are evaluated.
- Some, with amazing hindsight, argue that active management was—of course!—doomed to fail in this unprecedented, protracted environment of quantitative easing and global liquidity provided by central banks. In other words, low, and even, in some cases, *negative*, yields on low-risk investments such as Treasury

bonds incentivize investors to buy anything that looks set to out-perform the ~1 percent you can earn on a money market fund. The rising tide of liquidity has lifted all investment boats, goes this argument, and when the tide goes out, the passive strategies will be revealed as skinny-dippers.

- Some believe that passive investment management is undermin-ing the very essence of capitalism, which theoretically funnels capital toward the best return ideas. In a passive-dominated world, there are no stock pickers allocating capital, but, rather, an automated rebalancing program to make sure index weights are reflected. This argument has been taken a step further and suggests that passive strategies have led to systematic stock mar-ket overvaluation.[11]

- Finally, some believe that buying a passive strategy is like buy-ing the cheapest car on the new car lot. It won't have any of the safety features, such as lane departure warnings, automatic breaking, and side view cameras. While the road is flat, straight, and well maintained, the cheapest car will get you from point A to point B. But if it's raining outside, or if the road you're travel-ing has numerous potholes and lots of winding curves—that is, if markets are volatile—you'd opt for the vehicle with the added features that will help you safely navigate.

We are not here to take either side of this debate, although it should be noted that we both work for active investment managers, and we both hope to have PM roles for decades to come. We believe that there is room for both models of investment management, and that the rise of passive strategies will create opportunities for the best active managers, who will take advantage of idiosyncratic opportu-nities that can't be pursued using passive strategies. Although the debate has relevance to our subject matter, we hope that by the end of this book, we will have made the case that improving gender diver-sity in active IM could help to slow, or even reverse, passive IM's share gains.

What Are "Alternatives," and Should I Care About Them?

Our discussion thus far has focused on investments that anyone can purchase—in fact, mutual funds were designed to give everyone, not just very wealthy people, the chance to participate in the stock and bond markets. If you read the financial press, you've probably heard about lots of other types of investments, most of which are inaccessible to individuals. In fact, some are expressly marketed or limited to qualified institutional buyers (QIBs), which are institutional investors with at least $100 million to invest. No individual person, no matter how wealthy, can be a QIB. Among other things, a QIB designation presumes a higher level of knowledge and sophistication on the part of the buyer, be it a multigenerational family office, endowment, foundation, or pension plan. As a result, the alternatives we'll discuss next generally have fewer regulatory burdens than mutual funds, along with less disclosure and audited information, because the Securities and Exchange Commission (SEC) assumes that investors of this size are smart enough to do their homework.

Although you probably can't qualify as a QIB, you might be able to purchase a subset of alternative investments available to "accredited investors" (AIs). AI is a designation requiring you to have a net worth of at least $1 million, excluding your primary residence, or an annual income of at least $200,000. And you might own alternatives indirectly, even if you've never purchased one yourself. For example, if you are fortunate enough to have a pension, it is likely designated as a QIB and has allocated some portion of its funds to alternatives—so in effect you are participating in these other investment opportunities. Here is a brief overview of alternatives.

- *Hedge funds*: This is a catch-all term to describe a wide range of investment strategies. The original concept is embedded in the name: to hedge against something. The earliest hedge funds (the first one opened to investors in 1949) were generally intended to hedge against stock market declines, and there are certainly still lots of these around. But today there are more than 10,000 investment vehicles that call themselves hedge funds, and they do everything from shorting the stock and bond markets to positioning themselves to have zero correlation with a given market (so-called market-neutral strategies).[12] Hedge funds do all this while charging fees that we traditional active managers envy: hedge funds fees are calculated using a 2 and 20 model, whereby the manager gets paid a base fee of 2 percent of assets under management (versus an average fee below 1 percent for active managers), and then 20 percent of the investment gains on the portfolio over an index's performance. Like the fees of active managers, hedge fund manager fees have also been under pressure, with 1 and 10 becoming the new normal. (This still looks pretty good to traditional active managers, whose fees are compressing from their historical average 0.5 percent to 1 percent of AUM, and who don't participate in the upside of index-beating performance.)

- *Private equity (PE)*: This is exactly what it sounds like: a firm that buys businesses and then holds them as private companies, meaning that the shares are not listed on a public stock exchange. PE firms generally buy companies (most often through leveraged buyouts, or LBOs) and increase their profitability and returns to shareholders through cost cutting, operational improvements, and the magic of leverage, the "L" in LBO. Think about the difference between your return on equity if you put 10 percent down on a house versus 50 percent. When you sell the house for 120 percent of what you paid for it, the investors who put 10 percent down pocket 30 percent of the final proceeds after paying back the bank, making three times their original investment. The more conservative investor who puts 50 percent down receives 70 percent of the final proceeds, making a significantly lower percentage return on her money.
- *Venture capital (VC)*: Think of this as an early-stage version of private equity focused on companies at the beginning of their

lives, with tremendous growth potential and high risk. Most of the tech firms you know by name started as tiny companies with VC funding. VC firms generally expect two to three of ten investments to be home runs; that is, to return multiples of the initial investment. Another two to three are expected to return their capital or break even, and the bottom half will to go bust.

- *Quant funds:* These "black box" (i.e., difficult-to-understand) funds utilize algorithms, rather than people, to pick investments. Although these algorithms are created by people, the program, once written, makes decisions. Quantitative investing sounds very different from how we'll describe traditional active IM in the next chapter, which is sometimes called "fundamental IM," but the two investment methodologies have some overlapping philosophies, though they are applied differently. A traditional active IM analyst looks for a security that is trading at a lower value than what his analysis shows it is worth. A quant analyst is also looking for undervalued securities, but here the algorithm calculates the security's intrinsic value. Unlike a traditional analyst, a quant analyst does not meet with management teams to evaluate their competency. This might sound like an analytical deficiency, but it eliminates the human element in decision-making, which can be good (if it eliminates biases) or bad (if it eliminates intuition). Both approaches, be they quant or fundamental, are trying to forecast the future sales, earnings, and cash flows of a company and compare these with what the market appears to be forecasting to identify good investment opportunities.

The Future of Active Investment Management: Ex-Growth, or Emerging Growth Opportunities?

The past decade has been tough for our industry. Squeezed at the top line by the passive share shift and the expense line by rising technology, compliance, and other costs, active IM has experienced profit margin compression. Many industry participants fear that traditional active investing will continue to be squeezed from both directions by the investment vehicles discussed earlier: higher-cost, specialized hedge funds/PE/VC at the higher and wealthier end of the market, and low-cost, passive investment vehicles at the other end.

But it isn't all gloom and doom in active IM. Growth areas include the following:

- *Emerging markets investors*: Offering products to emerging market clients that are better aligned with their needs
- *Private market investing*: Offering investors access to a class of investment that historically they have been unable to access
- *Holistic portfolio management*: Using data management and technology to design portfolios for entire cohorts of investors; commoditizing and making available strategies to the mass market that were previously restricted to accredited investors and QIBs
- *Environmental, social, governance (ESG)/impact investing*: This type of investing focuses on a subset of companies that score well against various measures of corporate responsibility. Impact investing is a bright spot in active IM, and it's a lot harder to replicate in passive vehicles because of the research intensity. According to a survey by Morgan Stanley, "Millennials are twice as likely to invest in a stock or a fund if social responsibility is part of the value-creation thesis."[13] A report by Fidelity says "a majority of affluent millennials (77 per cent) and Generation X donors (72 per cent) indicated they had made some form of impact investment, such as investing in a publicly traded company with good social or environmental practices."[14] Among the baby boomer and older generations, the ratio was a mere 30 per cent.[15] Although there aren't good numbers on the size of the ESG market—estimates range from $3 to $30 trillion AUM— there is widespread agreement that impact investing will grow exponentially in the decade to come.

Accessing these growth areas could allow active investment managers to protect their fee revenue while better meeting the needs of their clients. But investment managers of the future will have to meet some high standards.

- Long term, superior, index-beating track record of investment results—this is the highest barrier to entry for new managers; it is hard to build and easy to destroy.
- Low cost base—particularly for passive managers.
- Strong infrastructure—which can be supported only through scale.
- A stable shareholder base—which relies on strong distribution channels—which can be difficult to balance with a low-cost base.
- An entrepreneurial spirit—active managers must maintain the investment styles and approaches that have created their competitive advantage while allowing them to evolve with structural changes to markets and client needs.

To summarize: active IM has been evolving since its inception—but "evolution" might shift to "revolution" over the next decade. It's no wonder that the stocks of many publicly traded IM firms have underperformed the S&P 500 over the last decade.

We hope that this chapter gave you a better perspective on the industry we're writing about and disabused you of the notion that the book is focused on investment banks or financial advisors or other parts of the investing supply chain that might be more visible or recognizable to you. You should now know the difference between the person you meet with quarterly or annually to go over your brokerage account and the people you're going to meet in the next chapter: PMs and analysts. We look forward to introducing you to our coworkers.

2

What Is a Portfolio Manager, and Why Would Anyone Want to Become One?

This is the best job in the world. We get to meet with interesting companies and smart people every day, whether it's smart management or smart investors.

—SANDY MILLER, SENIOR PORTFOLIO MANAGER,
APG ASSET MANAGEMENT US, INC.

Our description of the analyst and PM roles focuses primarily on our experiences working at large mutual fund companies. At the long tail of small investment firms (such as the one where one of us now works), with only a few employees, there is often no distinction between the analyst and PM role. Although there are many successful examples of small firms using this model, traditional IM maintains a clear line between the analyst and PM. As you will learn in this chapter, the two jobs are quite different, and the largest investment managers are fortunate to have the resources to offer, and hire for, two separate career paths.

Educating laypeople about the roles of analyst and PM is key to recruiting talented individuals into the profession. Our surveys of undergraduate and MBA pipelines asked students to indicate their level of agreement with the statement, "I understand how to become a portfolio manager." At the undergrad level, our survey showed that men describe themselves as 2.1 times more likely than women to understand how to become a portfolio manager. Even at the graduate level, of the students we surveyed who have chosen to pursue IM careers, men are 22 percent more likely to agree with the statement. People don't understand the job—and at the risk of stating the obvious, it's a lot less likely that you'll pursue it if you don't know what it entails. The section that follows is not only meant to provide the background you need to read this book; we also want to give you a perspective on a day in the life of an analyst/PM that makes you think, "This sounds like a fun job, and I could envision myself doing it."

To demystify these roles, humor us with an analogy. Investing is like a theater production. Let's call our production *Beating the Market*. There are clearly defined roles, which come together to create the production of a diversified, alpha-generating portfolio. In most productions of *Beating the Market*, being an analyst is like being an actor, and being a PM is like being a director. Though it's not the focus of this book, we should at least mention the production support staff behind the scenes: traders—they're the musicians, providing the lubricant to keep the portfolio moving from idea to idea; and the back office—providing wardrobe changes, makeup, compliance, legal, and so on.

It should come as no surprise that, as with actors and directors, the required skill sets for analysts and PMs are different, and at times contradictory.

The analyst role is knowing a lot about a few things so you have an industry or a couple industries and 30 or 40 companies you follow. You know everything that is necessary about those companies to make a decent investment decision. As a portfolio manager, you know five things about 300 companies. It's a bell curve—the same area under the curve is the same amount of intellectual capacity, but one requires you to be much more detail oriented. Analysts need a lot of information to come to an investment decision; to be a good portfolio manager, you need to be much more intuitive than that. (PM comment)

We'll start with the analyst role, because it's the typical entry point into the industry and the feeder path into the PM role.

A Day in the Life of an Investment Analyst

Describing the typical day of an analyst is tough—because there is no typical day. It's one of the qualities of this profession that makes it so attractive and one of the reasons the profession resonates with self-starters and self-motivators. All investment analysts *analyze* securities issued by companies, whether stocks or bonds. What does this mean in practice? Although there are as many ways to analyze a company as there are analysts, some aspects of the work are common across firms.

- *Financial analysis*: An investment analyst is expected to build and maintain, via quarterly earnings updates, an excel model for every company in her coverage universe. Analysts are assigned either a list of stocks to cover or an industry (such as consumer staples or industrials) to follow—these stocks collectively form an analyst's coverage universe. The model is generally constructed using publicly available financial statements, supplemented with commentary from earnings calls (which are quarterly updates from management to the analyst community). The amount of detail in that model, including the number of years of historical data and future forecasts, is subject to a lot of discretion and depends on the type of analysis (e.g., equity versus fixed income).

- *Industry analysis*: An analyst needs to develop a deep understanding of the industries she follows, as well as how a company
  is performing versus its peers—looking at differences in returns,
  margins, revenue growth rates, and more, which is referred to as
  "benchmarking."
- *Management and board review*: This includes both evaluating
  the management team, which runs the company, as well as the
  board of directors, which is responsible for the stewardship of the
  company. Ideally this information is obtained through meetings
  with the CEO and/or CFO, although the luxury of management
  meetings is too often reserved for the largest equity investment
  managers. This part of the analysis also incorporates compensation analysis—how is the management team being paid? Are
  their incentives aligned with yours?

The fundamental job of all analysts is to use the model just described
to determine the intrinsic value of a company's shares and/or bonds,
and to compare the valuation implied by that analysis with the company's current market value. If there is a gap, and if the analyst believes
that there are catalysts to close that gap, then she will pitch her idea
to PMs, usually at an investment meeting.

Because we have, collectively, almost a half century of investment analyst experience, we could talk about the job for the rest of
this book. For now, if you'd like to learn more about this career, we
encourage you to check any of the thousands of books that have been
written about the role of an analyst, going all the way back to the
seminal tome, *Security Analysis*, published in 1934.[1]

The Journey from Analyst to PM

This is just one analyst's experience of the journey from analyst to
PM, but we believe it reflects a typical IM promotion path at a large
investment manager. Here is Ellen's journey, in her own words.

I was at the top of my analyst game when I started thinking about becoming a PM. I'd taken on coverage of several large, high-profile sectors: retail, REITs, media. PMs listened to me—not just the ones in fixed income, who were my captive audience, but equity PMs as well, who sought a second opinion about their holdings or a perspective on an unloved stock that nonetheless generated enough free cash flow to pay a hefty dividend. I loved being an analyst because I loved being read and listened to—in essence, performing.

At its heart, the job of an analyst is, well, analysis—and I also loved doing this. Company research is like a jigsaw puzzle where you know you'll never have anything close to all the pieces. Success lies in finding as many pieces as possible, and with those, identifying the outline of the picture with a higher degree of confidence than what the sum of the pieces would suggest. The most important part of my job as an analyst was knowing the right questions to ask to fill in as much of the puzzle as possible. These questions might be answered by SEC filings, primary research (for example, visiting JC Penney stores to see if there are customers there), and/or meetings with company management. The questions have to be divided into two categories: "must know" before investing, and "nice to know" before investing. The second most important part of my job as an analyst was distilling what I thought into a bite-sized investment thesis for PMs who had a hundred other analyst reports to read or listen to—note, this discipline made me a better analyst.

Once I transitioned to PM, I spent a lot of time listening and reacting to other people's ideas and research, as opposed to speaking and creating my own. I became one of the directors of a diverse group of analyst performers who auditioned at biweekly investment meetings. I also became an analyst of human nature. When our oil and gas analyst issued a lukewarm buy (he once wrote that he was flogging an idea with a limp, wet noodle, I believe ironically), I put that into the same category as the high-conviction idea of our wireless analyst, who could bring himself to tears describing the beauty of Sprint's spectrum. I learned how to ask tough questions gracefully—call this production notes—and which analysts preferred to be asked those questions in the comfort of a closed-door office rather than in front of the broader investment team.

To echo Ellen, at its heart, the job of a PM is, well, portfolio management: assembling a diversified, but not "di-worse-ified" (i.e. *too* diversified), group of investments that complement *and* hedge one another. The word "portfolio" is partly based on the Latin word *folium*, which means "leaf or sheet." Before the advent of electronic clearing, ownership of securities was based on physical stock certificates, which meant that a PM was managing a collection of paper stock and/or bond certificates or a collection of "foliums." Although the way we evidence ownership has changed, via custodians rather than pieces of paper, the premise is still correct: a PM is responsible for selecting and managing a collection of investments—which might be stocks, bonds, or other securities—that she expects will generate returns in excess of a benchmark for her clients.

Analyst interaction is one pillar of portfolio management; translating those interactions into a portfolio that beats the market is the most important part of a PM's job. The second most important part of a PM's role is distilling what we think into a bite-sized investment thesis for clients, prospects, and consultants who have a hundred other investment manager reports to read and/or listen to.

A PM spends a typical day analyzing her portfolio, asking questions like these. What industries am I over/underweight relative to the benchmark? What are the primary risks of my positioning, and am I comfortable with their sizing? What large issuers do I *not* own—and is there a good reason for that, or did an issuer just get overlooked by the analyst? PMs also read a lot—internal analyst writeups, external "sell side" reports, and relevant industry publications. They ask questions of the analysts, often in investment meetings that are designed to facilitate these interactions and for the benefit of other PMs and analysts. They talk to the traders about opportunistic buys and sells and market moves. They attend company management meetings with analysts. PMs also make time for client service, whether in one-on-one client meetings or investor panels for the financial advisors who sell their funds.

The Career Analyst Path: Urban Legend?

Now that you know what the job titles mean, we'll take you behind the curtain to look at a much-debated topic: Is there such a thing as a career analyst path—that is, an analyst who does not want to transition to a PM? In most other industries and corporate hierarchies, there's a clear progression of career paths, often involving language like "associate" and "partner." In IM, this is murkier. Analysts and PMs are equally important to the investment process, but because there are a lot more analyst jobs than PM jobs, at many firms PMs are viewed as the analysts' bosses. In fact, at one of the firms we've worked for, the analyst hiring pitch included this: "You can make as much money being an analyst as a PM"—in contrast to competitor firms, where the transition to PM is, rightly or wrongly, often viewed as a promotion. Here's a representative comment from our primary research: "I think most people assume you haven't really made it in our industry until you're managing money [i.e., a PM]."

Corroborating this perspective is the fact that women are somewhat better represented in the ranks of analysts than PMs. It's hard to find good data, but a CFA Institute study puts female analysts at 14 percent of the total.[2] Only 10 percent of PMs are female,[3] meaning that fewer female than male analysts transition to PM. Investment management is by no means the only industry in which men are promoted more frequently than women, but it is one of the furthest behind in fixing that situation.

We will explore the reasons for this more fully in chapter 3; for now, we'll tease this discussion with a quote from one of our PM interviewees:

I've had women analysts work for me, and I'm not sure why very few of them have aspired to be portfolio managers despite being some of my strongest analysts. I would see women analysts in meetings and think, "She has the strength of her convictions, and she's done her homework. And that is the kind of person who should be ultimately thinking about being a portfolio manager." It takes a level of confidence, but on the other hand, there's nothing worse to me than a male analyst with bravado who hasn't done his work.

Transitioning from analyst to PM requires planning, positioning, and—crucially—self-advocacy, which many studies show comes more naturally to men. It requires mentors and sponsors—cheerleaders, even. Several interviewees echoed the common wisdom that "mentors are people who talk about you when you're in the room—sponsors are people who talk about you when you're *not* in the room." Becoming a PM requires both types of supporters, along with a healthy dose of self-confidence. Considering that some of you are reading this because you're at an early stage in your careers, in the next section we offer the following strategies for transitioning from an analyst to a PM role.

Going from Analyst to a PM: One PM's Roadmap

1. *Develop a promotion plan:* Although keeping your career on track is your responsibility if you want to move into that next role—be it upward or lateral—you should have a promotion plan. Take an honest assessment of your current skills, then look at the job you want and determine which skills you'll need to do that job, and, finally, do a skills gap assessment. Developing the skills you need to bridge the gap doesn't need to be expensive. Look around and see what is available at your company. You have to own your career—your career journey is employee driven but manager supported.

2. *Learn to see the forest from the trees*: As you move from analyst to PM, you need to learn to give the "elevator speech" about a investment rather than tell the entire story from soup to nuts. Even if you build your portfolio from the bottom up, you should be able to talk about the characteristics of the portfolio and how it might react in certain situations. Learning to see the forest rather than the trees means that you are aiming to see how individual names fit within the portfolio. For example, when the oil and gas downturn happened in 2015, it didn't just affect names in your energy bucket; it had broader implications for the suppliers, which many analysts (and even PMs) hadn't considered.

3. *Demonstrate your communication skills*: PMs need to be strong communicators. Many of our interviewees, and your coauthors, received media and presentation skills training when they were promoted to PM. An analyst who wants to be promoted to PM should try to get this training early. Developing strong communication skills won't just help you as a PM; it will also improve your ability to pitch your ideas as an analyst. A good PM doesn't just know her stuff, she knows how to communicate to clients about it. You have to become comfortable talking about your portfolio when things aren't going so well—that, rather than the good times, is often when your clients want to hear from you more often.

4. *Be comfortable relying on your analysts/team*: A PM moves from being a team member to becoming a team leader, which can be a difficult transition. As a leader you need to make decisions when not all the information is known. And in investing, you don't get the opportunity to run parallel experiments—no chance to "let me run track A and track B and see which works best." You need to learn to trust your analysts trust the information, make an informed decision, and then stick with it. To be a successful PM, you need to trust the work of your team. You won't outperform if you continually second-guess the recommendations of analysts. I've seen PMs who read the annual report of a company

before buying a stock that an analyst was recommending and then boast about reading the report rather than just the analyst's note. Some PMs suffer from an Achilles heel of having to come up with a recommendation themselves rather than from the analysts' research; this can undermine results.

5. *Acknowledge that it's more than just stock picking*: An analyst must have conviction in her ideas, but a PM must have conviction in her entire portfolio. It isn't just about single stock selection. A good stock picker isn't necessarily a good PM.

What Do Portfolio Managers Think Makes Them Good at Their Jobs?

In a report titled "Diversity in Portfolio Management," New Financial[4] laid out the top eight attributes for portfolio managers. We heard a lot of corroborating comments in our interviews and have included some below.

1. Numeracy
2. Intellectual curiosity
3. Analytical ability
4. Aptitude for learning
5. Right balance of confidence and humility
6. Ability to challenge and openness to being challenged
7. Courage of conviction
8. Communication

We asked successful PMs, "What does it take to be a successful PM?" The responses were varied, but there were some common themes that we think women should consider before pursuing the career.

- *Intellectual curiosity*: This includes love of learning about new industries, new companies, and new areas. Companies change, new technologies can destroy an industry or market (ever heard of a buggy whip manufacturer?), and new entrants can transform the way a market operates (ask retailers whether they have been "Amazoned"). "We're so lucky that we literally get paid to learn about different businesses. I often refer to this job as a racket because you're getting paid to do something interesting, and yes, there are obviously stressful and tedious parts of it. But if you like learning, if you like putting the pieces of a puzzle together, this job is amazing."

- *Ability to work in an unstructured environment*: One of our interviewees, Howard Marks, cochairman and cofounder of Oaktree, has written extensively about investing and the traits of successful investors. His description of the job does justice to its fun anarchy: "Investing is always different and changing. There's no right answer, and today's right answer might be a wrong answer tomorrow. There is a lot of randomness. If you don't like that, you should choose a job with a lot of certainty and precision, like a dentist or a civil engineer." We agree that every day is different whether you are an analyst or a PM. You never know what can happen that could change the investing landscape in ways that you might not be sure about.

  Let's take an example and daisy-chain it out: As you walk to your desk at 6:30 a.m. ET, you find out that a drone has taken out refineries and oil fields in Saudi Arabia. What does that mean for other refinery companies—will they grow faster than the market as they gain market share? How long will those gains last? And if the oil price spikes, what does that mean for the earnings of oil companies? What does a spike in oil prices mean for consumers— will they feel it at the pump? For how long? Where might they cut back other spending in order to be able to afford to gas up the car? Oh, and speaking of that—does this mean electric vehicles will get a leg up?

- *Communication skills*: PMs have a wide array of interactions, with three primary constituencies:

1. *Company managers*: This includes CEOs, CFOs, treasurers, division heads, and other leaders in an organization with whom PMs and analysts meet to find out about their business, its competitive advantage, where they have gaps in their product lines, where they are investing for growth, how they treat the environment, and their social agenda is. (As a side note, as much as companies need investors like us to provide capital for their businesses, it is often surprising how little they know about our business.)

2. *Clients*: If you work at a mutual fund company, expect to get trotted out to talk to consultants who sell your funds. If you work for an institutional money manager, you speak directly with your clients or the consultants who hired you. In both cases, you've got to be able to translate the themes and hard numbers of your portfolio into language that your end consumer understands.

3. *Your "team"*: As discussed earlier, PMs rely on the support of a wide array of people—analysts, traders, back office—to manage their portfolios. Being a PM is *not* a solo sport; you need people supporting you who have expertise in a multitude of areas. A PM is only as good as the weakest link in her team.

- *The right balance of confidence and humility*: This is echoed by some of our interviewees:

  > "You have to have humility and balance it with confidence in yourself.
  > I've had so many lucky breaks. I am fully in acknowledgment of the fact that I've been very lucky in a lot of ways."

- *Luck*: Hard work, analysis, and intuition are never quite enough for long-term superior results; luck plays a role as well. We will reiterate the oft-used quote, "Positive returns often happen at the intersection of hard work and luck." Good PMs have the confidence to take responsibility for their efforts and the humility to acknowledge the role that luck sometimes plays in investing.

- *Courage of conviction*: Here we will just let our interviewees speak for themselves (with a lot of emphatic, and empathetic, head-nodding!).

> You need to be open to being wrong all the time, but you have to stick with it and keep trying and be willing to stand alone.
>
> You can't look to other investors or the market to pat you on the back and signal you're doing the right thing.
>
> The typical way of seeing the world: if I work hard, things are going to turn out right. But in investment management, you have to be prepared to work hard, and things don't turn out the way you expect. Everybody has to have that resilience and stamina to say, "Well, I'm going to take this pain. I'm going to go and review what happened. I'm going to learn the lessons."
>
> You have to have nerves of steel and a stomach of lime.

How Are Portfolio Managers Compensated?

The final section of this chapter might be the most interesting to those of you considering the profession. Let's start with what you've probably suspected and what we mentioned in our prologue: investment management is a high-paying profession, and PMs have the opportunity to make a lot of money. There are lots of qualifiers, but if you end up at the right firm, deliver returns for your investors, and have the right incentive structure, the upside is enormous. According to the CFA Institute, in 2016, the average PM made $344,600,[5] but to some extent this understates the potential upside: in 2019, five hedge fund managers took home $1 billion in yearly compensation.[6]

A paper on PM compensation in the mutual fund industry[7] noted that despite interest in the structure of PM compensation, little is known about it, and most research focuses on the compensation of the mutual fund advisor—a completely different job. Lately there has been some pressure from regulators for better disclosure of compensation practices in investment management. Even without regulatory pressure, it's awkward to grill a CEO on equitable pay practices when you're making ten times what your assistant makes.

There are many publicly traded IM firms, and they are required by the SEC to disclose the compensation paid to their top five executive officers. However, our analysis of 2018 proxies of the top five investment management firms by market capitalization finds that most of the named executives are not PMs. And even if those executives have investment oversight responsibilities, their compensation plans as described in the proxies are more closely linked to corporate objectives or the rankings of their mutual funds.

PM compensation across firms is not standardized. The following discussion of PM compensation relies on "Portfolio Manager Compensation in the Mutual Fund Industry" (February 2018), reviews of the annual reports of publicly traded IM firms, and our own personal experience.

The compensation of a PM comprises one or more of the following elements:

- *Base salary and benefits:* Although some PMs do not receive base salaries, typically they are paid at least a token base salary.
- *Cash performance bonus:* For 79 percent of funds, PM bonus compensation is tied to the performance of the funds managed. The period over which fund performance is measured varies significantly, from one quarter to ten years.
- *Incentive compensation tied to firm profitability:* The compensation of approximately 50 percent of PMs is tied to the underlying profitability of the firm they work for. The investment manager's assets under management might or might not be a consideration.

Although these are typically smaller components of compensation, PMs also might receive mutual fund units, deferred stock, stock options, and/or pension contributions. Finally, about 30 percent of PM compensation is deferred.

As with PM compensation, little has been written about how equity research analysts are compensated. Based on our experience and compensation publications from industry organizations such as the CFA Institute, analysts are paid a base salary as well as a performance-based bonus. This bonus is usually tied to the performance of the analyst's underlying stock recommendations, as well as reviews from PMs who evaluate the analyst's contribution to their portfolio's performance (the timeliness of responses to questions, number of actionable ideas pitched, quality of the investment ideas that are pitched, etc.). Analysts' bonuses are typically lower than PMs', and their bonus as a percentage of their total compensation is generally lower as well.

The amount of variable compensation that a PM receives relative to her base salary can be significant. Roughly a third of firms that voluntarily disclose their ratio of fixed to variable compensation show PM bonuses representing over 200 percent of their base compensation. How does a PM earn this bonus? By outperforming her index. To use a simple example, let's say you manage a fund whose benchmark is the S&P 500. Your base salary is $200,000. In 2018, when the SPX index was down ~5 percent (net of dividends), you were flat (a zero return). You stand to earn a $400,000 bonus (two times your base salary) for not earning your clients any money in 2018. Of course, you didn't lose any of their money, either—so maybe you deserve that reward.

Tying compensation to investment performance is a double-edged sword. If a PM is trailing the index halfway through the year, she might be incented to invest in higher-risk positions to meet incentive compensation bonus hurdles (the proverbial "swinging for the fences" approach). If successful, both the fund shareholders and the PM win; the former get higher returns, the latter gets her bonus. If not, the losses are sustained by the funds' shareholders rather than the PM, since there's no such thing as a negative bonus. So, although compensation plans are designed to minimize agency conflict, this does not always work.

The Commonsense Interpretation of Bonus Comp Tied to Performance . . .

Bonuses tied to a PM's performance relative to a benchmark are conceptually similar to stock option awards for management teams. In theory, they align everyone's interests: PMs with clients, and C-suiters with shareholders. In practice, they can encourage excessive risk taking. As the Business Roundtable of U.S. CEOs starts to pay lip service to, and perhaps even take action on, stakeholder value—that is, the push for management to consider multiple constituencies rather than solely shareholders—perhaps the active IM industry will consider its own version of this practice. The irony of investor agitation for reducing the wage gap between the C-suite and the rest of the employee base is that IM is one of the worst wage gap offenders. As the *Financial Times* reports,[8] the industry's evolving structure—increasing passive share; increasingly complex portfolio construction strategies and tools that rely on multiple inputs; and, most glaringly obvious, the mismatch between agitating for lower CEO pay while you are banking multiples of your salary in bonuses—suggests that a rethinking of the bonus structure is long overdue.

. . . and How This Might Be Viewed Through a Gendered Lens

In an industry that rewards an individual's performance against a benchmark, wouldn't you think there would be lines of women raising their hands to participate in this type of objective compensation structure? Actually, studies have shown that when offered piece-rate compensation, which is functionally comparable to the small salary plus big bonus structure of many PM jobs, versus a fixed salary, women are more likely to choose the latter.[9] Additionally, based on our experience and that of our peers, although relative performance is a factor in determining analyst and portfolio manager compensation, it is not the only factor that goes into the bonus determination. And these other, nonquantifiable, factors and general lack of transparency around compensation at many IM firms make it difficult to understand exactly how PMs are compensated. To ask a deliberately provocative question, knowing that two-thirds of large-cap active managers don't outperform their benchmark,[10] why on earth should big bonuses be standard practice? The answer lies in these other, opaque compensation factors—which, as we will see, have the potential to discriminate against women in the same old insidious ways.

Conclusion: Now You Know What We Do, Right?

We hope that this chapter gave you a good overall view of the analyst and PM jobs. We don't believe you've encountered any differences in the job descriptions that suggest a physiological or temperamental reason that men might just be better at investment analysis or portfolio management than women. Whether they were male or female, the best PMs we've worked with and observed over the years have created an environment of constructive feedback, which made analysts feel comfortable expressing their ideas and open to thoughtful questions and different points of view.

We stole a bit of thunder from the next chapter, which digs into the headline gender numbers we cited earlier in this one. Our primary goal in this chapter is to demystify the jobs and to give you confidence that you, too, can become an analyst or PM if you enjoy the intellectual challenges we've just described. We'll leave you with a quote from a successful female PM:

> I can't think of a better job. I literally love going into the office every day. Really, it's the best job ever. You're constantly learning and growing.

We couldn't have said it better ourselves.

3

Representation of Women in
Investment Management

In this chapter we will present you with a lot of data about the lack of gender diversity in investment management and convince you of the need for our book—or you can ask for your money back. Many of the data sources we cite quantify other diversity deficits in the industry, which we hope someone will take up as the subject of another book. If you've ever read an article about investing, you know its central tenet: a portfolio with too few holdings and large, concentrated positions is high risk. Yet this is exactly how the industry has constructed its workforce. Our industry's lack of diversity is ironic, as diversification is the foundation of portfolio management.

Starting at the top of the funnel, the chart below shows the percentage of management positions in financial services by gender. The Governmental Accountability Office reports[1] show that progress has been made in increasing minority representation, but not female representation, in finance.

A study by Exane BNP Paribas corroborates this; it also found that women are less represented at the management level in the financial sector.[2] Although both of us work at firms with female CEOs, women run a very small number of IM firms.

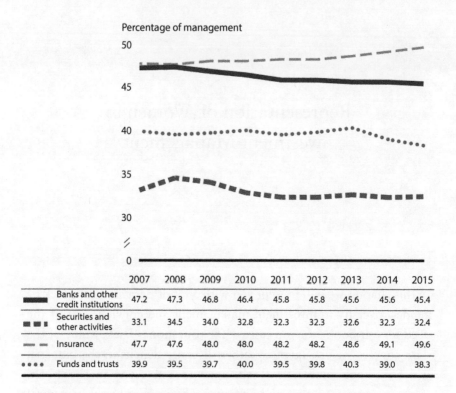

Percentage of management

	2007	2008	2009	2010	2011	2012	2013	2014	2015
Banks and other credit institutions	47.2	47.3	46.8	46.4	45.8	45.8	45.6	45.6	45.4
Securities and other activities	33.1	34.5	34.0	32.8	32.3	32.3	32.6	32.3	32.4
Insurance	47.7	47.6	48.0	48.0	48.2	48.2	48.6	49.1	49.6
Funds and trusts	39.9	39.5	39.7	40.0	39.5	39.8	40.3	39.0	38.3

FIGURE 3.1 Representation of women in the financial services industry by sector, 2007–2015.

Source: GAO Analysis of Equal Opportunity Commission Data, GAO 18–64.

IM's woman problem might have gotten less attention because it is hard to see exactly who is managing your money. As in many industries, there is relatively good gender parity in the marketing and client service arms of large fund managers. For example, the top fifty hedge funds—one of the least diverse investing segments—have achieved gender parity in their marketing and investor relations departments. However, those jobs pay less than the investing roles. The fact that your investment sales rep is female masks the strong likelihood that the PMs actually investing your money are male.

Portfolio Managers: We Are the Ten Percent

The headline number, from Morningstar's inaugural study of gender trends in money management (2015), is that "less than 10 percent of all U.S. fund managers are women"(table 3.1).[3]

Morningstar's study focuses on "open-ended U.S. mutual funds" and further breaks down the data into four categories (table 3.2).

Although other studies have reported slightly different results, they are similar in direction and slow to change. According to a CFA Institute survey of its members,[4] 15 percent of PMs are women. This number has remained stubbornly constant; in an update of the study that expanded the universe to the global investment management landscape, Morningstar found that little had changed in the United States or globally.[5] A study by Ignites corroborated Morningstar's, finding that "women got control of more industry assets during 2018, but still accounted for just 13 percent of all PMs added to mutual fund and ETF portfolios last year."[6] Further, the study noted that "the hiring [of female PMs] has been relatively concentrated. Some 62 percent of the 156 female PMs added to fund prospectuses during the first 11 months of 2018 work at just 11 fund complexes, data shows." And Citywire, an industry website and news outlet, reports as of year end 2019 that its database of more than 10,000 worldwide PMs is 10.8 percent female—up from 10.3 percent in 2016.[7]

TABLE 3.1 Fund managers by gender (%)

	Equity funds	Fixed-income funds
Women only	3	2
Total women-involved	24	20

Source: Laura Pavlenko Lutton and Erin Davis, *Morningstar Research Report: Fund Managers by Gender* (research report, Morningstar, 2015). Data as of March 31, 2015.

TABLE 3.2 Fund managers by gender and mutual fund type (%)

	Equity funds	Fixed-income funds	Allocation funds	Alternative	All funds
Women only	3	2	1	3	2
Men only	76	80	63	84	76
Women & men	21	18	37	13	21
Total women-involved	24	20	38	16	23

Source: Lutton and Davis, *Morningstar Research Report: Fund Managers by Gender*, p. 4.

Note: These numbers don't map to the 10 percent headline number, presumably because the "women & men" funds have less than a 50–50 female–male composition.

. . . Or Maybe Even the One Percent

The headline number is bad enough, but it understates the imbalance. Bella Research and the Knight Foundation found that only 0.9 percent of assets in the roughly $70 trillion U.S. investment industry is managed by firms that are majority owned by either women or minorities.[8]

But It's Like This in All High-Earning Careers, Right? No.

Morningstar points out,

Notably, the fund industry's leadership ranks are less-diversified than other comparable professions. A woman is less likely to be running a U.S. mutual fund than working as a doctor (37 percent), lawyer (33 percent), or accountant or auditor (63 percent). Women are also better-represented in law leadership ranks: 20 percent of law-firm partners are women, while 24 percent of federal judges are women. In accounting, 19 percent of partners in U.S. accounting firms are women.[9]

Knowing that one in three lawyers in the United States is female,[10] we asked a lawyer who ran a fund management company for his thoughts on this.

> Lawyers are more process-oriented people, and since women are generally more process oriented than men, the law profession is pretty gender balanced. There are fewer personality differences between the men and women who choose law as a profession, since anyone who chooses to become a lawyer is by definition process oriented. Lawyers are good at spotting issues, identifying the downside risk, and making complex things simpler—all skills that might skew more female. It isn't about work–life balance. Lawyers don't have time to golf. (Paul Haaga, retired chairman, Capital Research & Management Company)

Investing is comparable to engineering, a traditionally male-dominated industry. A recent study by Engineering UK found that only 12 percent of engineering functions are held by women.[11] The only industry we could find with less gender balance is—wait for it—real estate, in which only 4 percent of senior investment roles are held by women.

Medicine's Transition from Male Dominated to More Balanced (Job Sharing, Flexible Hours)

One of our former coworkers often broached the subject of job sharing in portfolio management using medicine as a precedent. As she wryly observed, managing the care of a patient is more demanding than managing money. You do, in fact, encounter life-or-death situations as a doctor; although we typically want to die when a holding goes bankrupt, thus far none of our mistakes has killed anyone. As a patient, wouldn't you prefer two opinions to one? And why should this be different for your portfolio?

No industry has cracked the code completely, but medicine comes close, thanks to structural changes that have offered women the kind of flexibility many women desire. Today medical school graduates are roughly half female, versus about 38 percent in MBA programs from 2012 to 2017.[12] "Female doctors are likelier than women with law degrees, business degrees or doctorates to have children. They're also much less likely to stop working when they do," according to Claire Cain Miller, who writes about gender issues for *The New York Times*.[13] Her research identifies one primary and one secondary driver of the profession's better gender balance:

1. *Flexible, predictable working hours*: Who wouldn't love this—besides misanthropes who don't want to spend time with their families? The image of the harried, ever-on-call doctor is dated. Today, rather than being practice owners, "doctors are much likelier to work for large group practices or hospitals and be on call at predictable times." The on-call hours of investment management are more predictable than patient management; the U.S. stock markets are generally open from 9:30 a.m. to 4:00 P.M. Eastern time, although trading in some asset classes, such as bonds, does take place outside those hours. Of course, a substantial amount of work also takes place outside these hours—but much of that work, such as portfolio analysis and earnings updates, can be done any time. In other words, IM *could* be flexible—but only if that is a key element of the workplace culture, which is not the case. To quote one study, "[MBA] women may also fall behind because of the career-family conflicts arising from the *purportedly* long hours, heavy travel commitments and *inflexible schedules* of most high-powered finance and corporate jobs"[14] (emphasis ours).

2. *Specialty options*: As anyone who has tried to get a gynecologist to diagnose plantar fasciitis knows, there are lots of different kinds of doctors—and hours vary by specialty. Cain Miller's research shows a correlation between average hours per week

and male:female ratios. Lower-hour specialties, such as dermatology and pediatrics, tend to have more women, whereas higher-hour specialties, such as cardiovascular medicine and surgery, are more male dominated. IM is similar to medicine in its trend toward greater specialization; compare the Warren Buffett days of looking at the whole universe of stocks with Fidelity's nine categories of U.S. stocks and twelve sector-focused fund categories, not to mention the fixed-income universe, which features a dozen or more discrete asset classes (Treasuries, mortgages, asset backed, corporates, high yield, leveraged loans . . . and that's just in the United States). Although there are definitely perceptions about the intensity of the various types of money management (e.g., equity PMs always think they work harder than bond PMs), we've never heard female MBAs chatting in the halls of Columbia Business School about how they're choosing a sector of investment management with lower intensity or more flexible hours. If you say anything other than "I stand ready to work 80 hours a week" in investment management interviews, you are not going to get a job.

Medicine holds valuable lessons for many industries, including IM. "The old market expectation that your doctor will be available at all hours and is entirely flexible was beginning to fall apart as the work force became more diverse," said Robert Wachter, chair of the Department of Medicine at the University of California, San Francisco. "If employers are serious about improving gender diversity in their workforce, they might want to think seriously about how they are structuring their jobs," says economist Melanie Wasserman (quoted in this article). As Cain-Miller, and our former coworker, point out, surely if your doctor can have work–life balance, your portfolio manager can, too.

Performance-based evaluation criteria are supposed to cure diversity problems . . .

The good thing if you're a woman or an underrepresented minority is you have stuff to point to because part of the problem with women and underrepresented minorities is that they are held to different standards than men.

One of the reasons for writing this book was our naive assumption that an industry in which performance is measured should be friendlier to women and minorities. Yet the statistics clearly prove otherwise, setting up an interesting tension between what the industry says it does—promote and pay based on performance—and what is actually happening. We heard this tension echoed by many of our interviewees. As you will see throughout this book, some of the quotes are directly attributed to the interviewees and some are anonymous. This is not to protect the guilty but, rather, for us to be able to provide you with a more balanced view of the investment management industry. Here are some representative quotes about women in IM (with emphasis added by your authors).

It *should* be a very good career for women—you have metrics to measure performance—there *shouldn't* be room for politics.

I thought I was in a meritocracy, and results should have spoken for themselves.

One of the fascinating things about this business—it should in theory be one of the easier businesses to be gender neutral because you have performance numbers. Yet one of the things that utterly astounds me is the number of times that people don't look at data.

... But They Don't

A paper by Barber, Scherbina, and Schlusche[15] found that even in a transparent and performance-oriented culture, observable biases against some employee groups persist, particularly regarding women. And in this type of culture, these biases are likely to be worse than in others. The very reason that we thought more women would be attracted to investment management—a reason we heard from some of our interviewees—might in fact be working against women, not for them. Perhaps the more challenging perspective for women in IM is not the infamous quote from a very successful hedge fund founder ("You will never see as many great women investors or traders as men. Period. End of story."). Rather, it's the many senior-level men at investment management firms who say some version of "I don't see gender, I just see numbers" when they talk about the lack of diversity at their firms. As an interesting side note, our survey of MBA students committed to IM jobs found that women are 16 percent less likely than men to view IM as a meritocracy—a well-founded gap in perception.

Alpha Males Don't Generate Alpha: An Overview of Studies Comparing Female and Male Investment Performance

Let's begin this section by admitting that it almost didn't make it into our book. Our thesis is not that women are better investors than men but, rather, that there is no gendered component of investing that makes men more intellectually suited to it. We won't sink to the level of quoting chat boards here, but suffice it to say that a vocal minority of men contend that investing should be left to them.

You might be wondering, why would we exclude whatever data we had if the numbers support the view that women generate returns as good as or better than men? The answer: self-selection and survivor bias, two closely related but distinct phenomena that could skew results. A study published in the *Journal of Accounting Research* found that female equity analysts' recommendations outperformed those of their male peers. The study's author attributes this to self-selection bias: that is, there are so many males in the industry that only a woman with above-average abilities would choose this profession.[16]

The author notes that other studies show that women are less competitive and more risk averse than men—but in this study, women's superior performance is attributed to their bolder and more accurate forecasts.[17] This corroborates self-selection bias; only women who overcome the typical female deficits in competitiveness and risk appetite—who are confident enough to make these so-called bolder forecasts—sign up for a career that demands such forecasts.

Taking this analysis to its natural conclusion, more women would reduce the female returns, as they would dilute the pool of true superwomen with their more average counterparts. But this "diluting the pool" excuse for the lack of diversity in IM makes no sense to us from a purely statistical perspective. Take two groups: a group of 100 women and a group of 100 men. Each group has a 50 percent chance of delivering returns above the index and 50 percent below the benchmark, with identical standard deviations. If you choose the top 10 women from the female group and the top 90 men from the male group (aka almost all of them!), the returns of the entire group will be slightly above the mean of the two separate groups but not significantly greater with a fairly similar standard deviation of returns. But consider the situation in which you took the top 50 percent from each group—that is, the top 50 men and the top 50 women. The mean of that new gender-balanced group will be significantly higher than the mean of either the women-only or the male-only group. Yes, we know that 40 men are now out of jobs, with their positions being taken by women, but as we said in the prologue, this is a profession that pays well, and women are as entitled to participate in these financial rewards as are men.

Survivor bias poses a related challenge when interpreting results by gender. Given that it is demonstrably harder for women than men to become, and remain, PMs, the ones who succeed are likely to produce very good results—possibly much better than those of their male peers. Although we have argued that our industry is not a pure meritocracy, despite its fixation on performance, very high returns relative to peers and benchmarks don't get overlooked. So we should be skeptical about studies of male versus female PMs because it's possible that the women included in such studies (a) have the more "male" attributes that investing is known for and fit in well with their white, alpha-male peers, and/or (b) have been such good investors that even their gender could not hold them back.

Finally, we heard in our primary research that women who succeeded in IM sometimes started, and often stayed, in smaller, more eclectic, even "backwater" asset classes, such as international and small-cap stocks. In other words, they took the jobs that men didn't want, because they were committed to the PM career path. These unloved areas have proven more "alpha-rich" than the traditional plum jobs (e.g., large-cap U.S. stocks), meaning that it is easier to beat the benchmark. If women are disproportionately managing alpha-rich sectors, they will de facto have better results. The most recent example of this is the area of socially responsible and impact investing, which is at gender parity—likely because, until stakeholder capitalism, climate change, and other "woke" concepts started to trend, men didn't want to do it.[18]

Selection and survivor bias aside, in the spirit of doing our research (just as we do at our day jobs), we include the relatively few industry studies that compare the performance of male and female investment returns—many of which show that women deliver higher returns with less risk than their male counterparts.

The inaugural study (to our knowledge, anyway) of male/female performance trends was published in 2001 and analyzed returns of 35,000 households from 1991 to 1997.[19] So, caveat: this study did not focus on professional investors but, rather, everyday people with accounts at an unidentified discount brokerage. The study found a small but meaningful difference in returns between men and women; women outperformed by 94 bps per year, which doesn't sound like a lot—until you factor in compounding.

The authors identified one simple difference in male/female portfolios that accounted for the return differential: trading frequency. "Women turn their portfolios over approximately 53 percent annually, while men turn their portfolios over approximately 77 percent annually." Excessive turnover and trading has been shown in many studies to be detrimental to returns, even when adjusting for transaction costs. The authors attribute this to overconfidence: "Psychologists find that in areas such as finance men are more overconfident than women."[20]

More recently, Morningstar studied this question and concluded that "the hypothesis that men outperform is not supported."[21] The study found "no significant difference between female and male [equity] managers"—and to the extent there was a difference, it was in favor of women: "Over five years, the typical all-women team produced [equity and fixed-income] returns that were 0.41 percent and 0.38 percent annually above the category average, respectively." With the caveat that collateralized loan obligations (CLOs) are an esoteric, small asset class, a Citigroup study analyzing data from 2013 to 2018 found that female CLO managers outperformed male managers.[22] And we would be remiss not to include preliminary pandemic results: a Goldman Sachs study of 500 equity mutual funds found that those with at least one third female PMs beat those with no women by 100 bps as of August 26, 2020. (The study reported no gendered difference in results in the prior three years.)[23]

Hedge funds, which are even more male dominated than traditional IM firms, have also shown a clear trend of female outperformance—but here again, the sample size is so small that it's difficult to read much into the numbers.[24]

Another Take on Results: Diverse Teams Don't Deliver Better Performance. . . At Least, Initially

When the CFA Institute conducted diversity and inclusion workshops and asked participants to identify the top three reasons for advocating for diversity and inclusion, 80 percent of them listed improved business outcomes.[25] And that, in fact, is one of the pillars of our investment thesis, so to speak, for the industry: increased diversity can halt its decline. You can imagine our surprise and dismay when we found out that adding women to an investment team resulted in a decrease in performance—at least initially. Bär, Niessen-Ruenzi, and Ruenzi found that gender diversity in teams had a significant negative impact on performance.[26] Similarly, the CFA Institute found that social categorization diversity within teams (which mostly means gender diversity) "leads to decreased within-group communication, and team performance is eventually negatively affected."[27] Having women on the team also led to less cohesion and lower levels of satisfaction.

There is hope, however. The first study noted that the likely reason for the lower results was the very small representation of women. Investment management suffers from a "salient minority" effect—that is, when women (or any minority) are a small, token component of a team, without enough critical mass to influence decision-making or results. The threshold level for a salient minority is generally thought to be around 30 percent. In another study evaluating a female-dominated group, there was no impact of gender diversity on performance. The study's authors observe that "the negative effect of gender diversity might vanish if the share of women employed actually rises to a level where women are not a salient minority."[28]

There is also good news about diversity in the C-suite, which has implications for any industry with salient minorities. Although adding women to an all-male board could initially have negative returns, at a critical mass of 30 percent,[29] diversity leads to improved company performance compared with performance in a company with an all-male board.[30] Given that women are considered to be better communicators (men are better in monologue, whereas women are better at dialogue),[31] more inclusive, and more likely to share information than men, having more women could result in better intra-group communication than in an all-male team. In other words, more women equals more returns.

Here's a problem, though. The CFA Institute found that 70 percent of its female members believed that having a team composed of both men and women delivered better investment results—but only

43 percent of men thought so.[32] With over 90 percent of the senior management roles at IM firms held by men, and the majority of men holding the opinion that gender-diverse teams do not result in better performance, a better case needs to be made for diversity. Yet the chicken-and-egg effect applies here: if adding a woman or two to an investment team actually dampens performance, the push for gender parity stagnates—right at the inflection point where this salient minority needs to evolve into a meaningful one in order to achieve better results.

ESG/Impact Investing—How Do Investment Managers Stack Up in Their Own Screens for Good Stakeholder Practices?

We'll conclude this session by turning the tables on the IM industry. You've doubtless seen the headlines, but in case you haven't, here is a representative sample:

Investors Should Look Beyond the Bottom Line (*Financial Times*, October 21, 2019)
We Need a New Capitalism (*New York Times*, October 14, 2019)
Move Over, Shareholders: Top CEOs Say Companies Have Obligations to Society (*Wall Street Journal*, August 19, 2019)

It might be an overstatement to say that Jamie Dimon, the CEO of JP Morgan, started it all. But when the Business Roundtable that he chairs came out in favor of stakeholder rather than shareholder capitalism, it seemed like the trickle of requests for ESG and/or SRI portfolios (environmental/social/governance and socially responsible investing, respectively) turned into a flood. The concept of investing in companies that treat all their constituencies with respect and fairness is moving quickly from niche into the mainstream.

In response, many investment managers are integrating ESG analysis into their investment process. We decided to look at how the IM industry itself scored through an ESG lens. The FTSE Russell studied the percentage of women on boards by sector globally as well as the social pillar score of the sector. The financial sector ranked third behind telecom and utilities in terms of its ratio of women to men on boards. But it was the bottom performer in terms of its "social pillar score," which measures how well a company is managing social impact and risks in five areas—labor standards, human rights, supply chains, customer responsibility, and health and safety—across more than one hundred indicators.

The conclusion is that although we are good in the boardroom, the industry has an abysmal social pillar ranking. As one of our (male) interviewees admitted, "It's a shitty, grubby business." We think that this could be contributing to the lack of women wanting to enter the industry in the first place—which we discuss later in this book. But even with what you've learned up to this point about the industry, if you were a CFO sitting across from a (likely pale) male PM demanding that your company bring its workforce to equal pay or gender parity, wouldn't you suggest he look in the mirror?

In the next section of the book, we will do just that: hold a mirror up to our collective face. You know the scope of IM's woman problem; now it's time to turn to the reasons behind it.

PART TWO

Diagnosis of IM's Gender Imbalance

Introduction

By this point you should have gained an understanding of the structure of the investment management industry and the job description of a portfolio manager and an analyst. Additionally, you're now well-versed in the numbers and statistics that led us to write this book: the dearth of women PMs, which is not replicated across other high-earning fields such as medicine and law. You'll hear lots of different perspectives in the next six chapters, where we will diagnose the problem along several points in the PM pathway. We will go back as far as the undergraduate pipeline and then graduate school, where we focus on MBA programs, the most traditional educational feeder into IM. Finally, we'll look at various inflection points along a PM's career path. This section draws on a wealth of primary research from more than a hundred interviews with undergraduate and graduate students and current and former industry practitioners. We don't want to lead you to one conclusion; rather, we'll let these myriad voices create a narrative with room for multiple interpretations.

Debunking the Myths

Before we dive into the results and implications of our interviews and research, we need to address some commonly held views of IM. Call this "Why people *think* women don't choose to become PMs." We've found that many industry practitioners are wed to some of the following myths about the profession. Although some of them apply to specific firms or specific segments of IM, for the most part they are exactly that, myths. Of course, this mythology can become self-fulfilling, as women unfamiliar with the nuances of the role self-select away from it. But we hope that our book can help to debunk the following misconceptions about the PM role.

- *Work–life balance is impossible to achieve as a PM.* Investing is a demanding job, but it's not a billable hours job like law, and it's less client oriented than the sell side. In fact, some of the successful PMs we interviewed chose the PM role because it enables them the flexibility to have greater work–life balance than they would have in other professions. Although we did hear some of the typical stories about sending trading orders from the delivery room and pumping breast milk between client meetings, the most representative quote on this subject is heartening: "I have literally never known a woman PM who quit because she couldn't figure out how to balance having children and having her career." The good news for those of you thinking about this career is that the families of successful women PMs come in all shapes and sizes, including married-to-jobbers ("I don't have kids, I have cats"), women married to stay-at-home-dads (SAHDs?),[1] dual-income households, and divorced and/or single moms. The SAHD PMs often mentioned their supportive home-husbands as a component of their success, but they generally described this as a luxury rather than a necessity. We did hear from one [male]

PM that "running a portfolio is pretty much all-consuming. So, it's very difficult to reconcile with other personal goals such as having a family." But his perception is different from the lived reality of many of our interviewees. We've chosen to devote an entire chapter to debunking this myth because we think it's so important.

- *Men are constitutionally better suited to the profession; good investors have male personality traits.* Men have no chromosomal advantage in IM—recall from chapter 3 that the small number of studies comparing male and female returns show that women are at least as good as, and in some cases slightly better than, men when it comes to delivering superior, indexing-beating investment returns. And some personality attributes more typically associated with men and testosterone (overconfidence, aggression) are inconsistent with superior long-term results.

- *There aren't any role models.* Yes, it would help if aspiring female PMs had more female role models, and we are heartened by some recent efforts to increase the visibility of female PMs in the industry. But law and medicine also lacked female role models when the transition to gender balance began, and somehow those industries slowly but surely evolved to achieve gender parity. Our constellation chapter provides the perspectives of PM role models for aspiring PMs.

- *Investing requires intensive math skills.* We know from studies that girls suffer more of a confidence deficit in their math abilities than boys, and this bias persists throughout secondary education.[2] We can tell you from personal experience that quant skills are not the primary drivers of outperformance. Many students, both men and women, new to the investing world who brave Ellen's investing classes (Ellen is an adjunct professor at Columbia Business School) are surprised by how little math is involved. As one of our interviewees said, "If your job isn't 'quant' (aka writing algorithms), then you only need sixth-grade math to succeed." Your authors' academic and career experiences corroborate this: one of us is a literature major who never learned how to work her HP calculator during business school, and the other holds a degree in computer science. As you'll read in chapter 9, the literature major was so turned off by the idea that her job would require a lot of math that she went into it with a one-year commitment, promising herself, "I'll give this job a year to prove that it's fun, and if it's all boring spreadsheets, I'll do something else." It's not just non-math majors that the industry risks alienating—it's anyone who doesn't want a quant job.

- *The "Wolf of Wall Street" is a real dude, who will be my boss, and I'll have to smoke cigars and play golf to fit in.* We'll explore this image issue more in the next chapter, but for now, we will leave you with a quote from an article Ellen penned in the *Financial Times*:[3] "I've encountered more asexual introverts in the course of my career than lecherous gropers. No one has ever put an exploratory hand on my arse. The aggregate culture of my workplaces has been as far from 'oversexualized' as *Sesame Street* is from *The Wolf of Wall Street*." This perception was confirmed by our interviewees; here is a representative quote: "I've never had a #metoo issue." The men in our industry might manage money for movie stars, but that is as close as this industry gets to these Hollywood stereotypes.

There are, of course, other perceptions of the industry that put off women that have some grounding in reality, and we'll talk about them in the chapters to come. But for now, please banish images of Michael Douglas as Gordon Gekko and Leonardo DiCaprio in *The Wolf of Wall Street* from your mental dictionary entry for "portfolio manager."

Although it's true that the image above captures much of the historical PM demographic . . .

. . . we suggest replacing this stock photo (no pun intended!) with this next one as you think about who should manage your money.

She might be a better investor than the guys are.

A Note About Our Primary Research

In the spring of 2019, we began compiling a list of women and men in the industry to interview. We found that not only were women interested in talking about gender diversity on Wall Street, but they also wanted to refer us to other women. Reactions from men were more balanced; fewer of them were willing to speak on the record. Their views are still reflected here, as are discussions with male and female peers we've had throughout our careers. Neither diagnosis nor—importantly—solutions can take place in an echo chamber of all-female voices. To affect change, men must be part of the conversation.

You'll hear the unfiltered comments of women who have succeeded, struggled, and soared in an industry with very few "sisters" to sponsor them. As you'll see, this doesn't mean they had zero support; many of them had support networks that included men and women. To avoid survivor bias, we have included a few voices of women who opted out of the industry, either very early (at the MBA level), on the way to becoming PMs, or via early retirement (voluntary or involuntary).

Finally, before we introduce you to our peers, we would like to highlight one theme of our primary research—one that is not industry specific but, rather, gender specific: humility. The phrases "good timing," "fortunate," "grateful," and—most of all—"luck" came up often. The following quote captures the attitude of many of our interviewees as they reflected on their career success: "The best word to sum up my career: lucky."

We mention this for two reasons. First, it's unlikely that those words would have appeared with such regularity in a random sample of successful men in the industry. (We hypothesize that "hard work" would likely replace "luck.") Second, in the words of a successful investor who echoed the words of a famous philosopher, good returns happen when hard work meets luck. *Investing lies at the intersection of luck and hard work.* As a PM, you could be as lucky as a leprechaun, but if you aren't prepared to take advantage of the opportunity because you haven't done the work up front, those opportunities will pass you by. Failure to acknowledge luck as a contributor to any successful PM's career is disingenuous and, arguably, arrogant.

Yet the current culture of IM can lionize overconfidence. The confidence cult created by superstar PMs has no room for luck; to let it creep into the discussion risks damaging this highly compensated male cult. We will dig more deeply into the concept of confidence and its relevance to investing in the following chapters. For now, we leave you with a question spawned by this quote from the authors of an entire book on the subject, *The Confidence Code*:

> Columbia Business School even has a term for it now. They call it "honest overconfidence" and they have found that men on average rate their performance to be 30 percent better than it is.[4]

How can an industry that rewards confidence accommodate a gender that errs on the side of "honest underconfidence"? As you read this section, we hope to give you an honest perspective on this key issue from women across the IM career spectrum.

4

Why Don't Women Choose Investing Careers?

The Undergraduate Pipeline

Although most analyst positions are reserved for MBAs, which we discuss in more detail in the next chapter, some IM firms start recruiting
employees for entry-level analyst roles while they're still in college.
Therefore, this chapter seeks to understand the barriers at the earliest
stage of the IM pipeline. As PMs we have learned how to collaborate,
and this chapter is the result of a joint effort between the authors and
a team of Rutgers University folks led by Professor Lisa Kaplowitz
with support from students Osayre Gomez, Ty-Lynn Johnson, Emanuel Marques, and Bernadette McCormick.

Let's start with some basic statistics on college degrees by gender. More women than men earn college degrees; the ratio of degrees
awarded to women has hovered around 57 percent over the prior
decade, and women earn 28 percent more undergraduate degrees
today than a decade ago.[1] Even within the narrow field of business,
representing 19 percent of degrees awarded, the female representation
is still close to 50/50 (yes, we rounded up from 47 percent).[2] Digging
into the data, we found that finance degrees, which represent only
2 percent of undergraduate degrees, have less gender balance, with
only 29 percent awarded to women. And the trend is moving in the
wrong direction—this percentage has declined by 5 points over the

past decade. Although a finance or business degree is not a prerequisite for an entry-level job in IM (and, in fact, some firms love to hire liberal arts grads for their intellectual horsepower), it is certainly not a good sign that fewer women are choosing to major in finance, a natural feeder into an IM career.

We've been working in finance for decades and will admit to having preconceived notions about why young women don't pursue investing careers: finance's bad image, the Hollywood effect, and the perception of the job as math oriented.

Finance's Bad Image: Is It the Next Target for Greta Thunberg?

According to a 2017 study,[3] the finance industry ranks third among the least trustworthy industries in the United States (not a bronze medal that we should be proud to receive). The worst? Oil and gas—no surprise given increasing concerns about global warming. For an even more damning report, the Edelman Trust Barometer found that finance ranked *below* oil and gas—in its study, we won the gold.[4] And with such a terrible image, we understand why no bright young idealistic Gen-Z or iGen woman wants to tell her friends and family she's going to work on the dark side—that is, for an investment manager. Most ordinary people don't have a working knowledge of what we do; it's not like this job is as well known and understood as, say, that of a doctor or lawyer. Most laypeople lump us in with the Wall Street crowd—the guys (always guys) who foreclosed on them or their parents or their next-door neighbor or their best friend during the financial crisis and received bailout packages for doing so. Even our own friends and family are generally fuzzy on the details of our day-to-day lives. One of our lawyer friends, who was valedictorian of her law school class (not an uneducated person!), likes to say, "Ellen works in money," when describing what we do.

Our industry seems to have an even worse image than technology among young women, which is notorious for its "bro" culture. As one of our interviewees said, "My sixteen-year-old niece wants to go to Silicon Valley because she's bought into the lifestyle—you know, free cafeteria, jeans." IM firms might have relaxed their stodgy dress codes, but the negative association remains, even if one of us is now allowed to wear jeans to the office and gets free lunch.

Big finance companies are catching on to this problem and agree that investment managers need an image makeover. Representatives from several financial services firms have stated publicly that negative perceptions of the industry could limit potential candidates' interest in the field. After exhorting the Business Roundtable he chairs to consider all of its stakeholders (rather than just its shareholders), JPMorgan Chase CEO Jamie Dimon highlighted the company's investments to help revive Detroit.[5] Showcasing how capitalism can be used to support good causes and not just make the rich richer is a good start (although it shouldn't be overlooked that Jamie Dimon is one of those rich people).

Gordon Gekko Was the Worst Thing for Gender Diversity in IM

We all remember Gordon Gekko's "greed is good" speech from the movie *Wall Street*—which left many people with a white alpha male as the dominant image of Wall Street professionals. Following his lead years later is *The Wolf of Wall Street*, another hard-charging, drug-taking, sexist white male Wall Street role model. And let's not forget that movie *The Big Short*, in which you can find members of our industry doing research in strip clubs.

It's not just women making this observation; the (male) CIO of CalSTRS, one of the largest pension plans in the United States, said, "Hollywood movies have given our industry a terrible image."[6]

Research has shown that when artifacts in an environment are culturally associated with the dominant group—in our industry, the white men of Wall Street—there is greater bias in decision-making.[7] Hollywood has given the IM profession some dubious artifacts—sex, drugs, and money. If your image of IM were formed by these movies, how would *you* feel about your daughter going to work at an IM firm?

Even if you step away from the silver screen, there are other widely circulated representations of investment professionals that inform female perceptions of the industry. The media is always happy to write articles with headlines like "Hedge Fund Bro Gonna Hedge Fund Bro"[8]—this is from the *Financial Times*, not a tabloid. One study of the technology industry, which we feel is a good proxy for IM, as both are knowledge-based professions with similar gender imbalances, found that women were much less likely than men (37 percent versus 56 percent) to believe that they were "culturally aligned" with the image of a successful tech worker.[9] Like female tech workers who don't see themselves in Mark Zuckerberg or Bill Gates, women in finance might also find it difficult to match themselves to the image of a successful Wall Street investment professional, or hedge fund bro.

You Need to Know Basic Math—But It's Less Than Half the Job

Related to perceptions about what an investor looks like, people outside the industry often believe that investing requires a lot of math. Numerous studies show that females are perceived to be worse at math than they are at other, so-called softer tasks, such as speaking and writing. Maura Cunningham, founder of Rock the Street, Wall Street, found that "in the U.S., we start to lose girls in math at age nine. As they age, girls report significantly lower confidence in math, despite earning equal scores to boys." We said it earlier, and we reiterate it here: you don't need to have taken calculus I, II, and III to succeed in IM—eighth-grade algebra will do just fine. The day-to-day tasks of an analyst and PM don't involve nearly as much math as you might think. But without exposure to people (women) who are actually doing the job, it can come across as highly quantitative, which alienates not just nonmath majors but anyone who shudders at the thought of spending most of her time in front of a spreadsheet running regression analyses and building complex forecasting models that integrate Walmart parking lot data and next-quarter sales forecasts. (Please, no.)

The Undergraduate Experience: Survey Results Confirm Our Hypotheses About Why Young Women Don't Pursue IM Careers

We are grimly happy to report that our hypotheses about why young women don't choose to work in IM were affirmed by a survey of undergraduates conducted by Lisa Kaplowitz and her students.[10] A few consistent themes emerged from their undergraduate research.

- Women view investing as a male-dominated profession—and are more likely to hold that view than men.
- Women are less likely than men to consider investing as a career path.
- Women are less knowledgeable than men about the industry and the jobs available to them.
- Women are less confident than men in their ability to land one of those jobs.

As we explored each of these issues from the undergraduate perspective and compared the attitudes of undergraduate males and females, we heard one theme frequently: exposure to women in IM—whether as friends, family members, professors, guest lecturers, or mentors—is critical in attracting female undergraduate talent. Because it is so important, we come back to this theme often in the next few pages. We will provide some concrete recommendations to address the importance of exposure to women PMs, along with showcasing some organizations that focus on it, in the solutions section.

Undergraduate Women See the Profession as Male-Dominated

Undergraduates perceive investing as a male-dominated profession, with 74 percent of women holding this view compared with 51 percent of men. This early perception is reinforced by some of the undergraduate finance and investment clubs on campus. These clubs often bring in guest speakers and industry experts to talk to students about life after college and what it is like to work in various fields. Given the statistics from the prior chapter, it is nine times more likely that these guest speakers will be men than women. A female sophomore student described her experience this way:

> I was so intimidated and felt so behind the eight-ball because I was not aware of the early identification programs and summer deadlines for internship applications. By sophomore year, the competition was so intense that I did not think there was a place for me in the finance candidate pool.

After participating in just one (male-dominated) finance club meeting, this student not only opted not to join the club, but she decided not to major in finance.

Another student commented on her experience in the classroom:

> Being raised by a mom who had a successful career in finance, I never thought that there was something I couldn't achieve because of my gender. It wasn't until I got to college and was one of the few women in my finance classes that I found myself doubting

my abilities solely because I didn't look like my peers or the guest speakers from the industry that came into our class.

Although many women identified with the statement, "investing is a male-dominated profession," our research shows that if a woman observes another woman in a senior-level finance role, it increases the student's belief that she can achieve the role herself. As one student recalled,

> The most impactful moment was when I heard a Latina woman speak on a panel, explaining her journey and accomplishments. She said, "I want to be the most influential Latina in banking." That has resonated with me to this date because now I aspire to be just like her. In fact, it was this quote that inspired me to join what seemed to be the most daunting table in the room—Investment Banking, even though I had no clue what that was.

One female student summed up the feeling of not-belonging well: "If the only stories that you know are of people that aren't anything like you, don't have any experience like you, don't look anything like you, don't remind you of anything about yourself . . . then you kind of think, is this really for me?" The accounts of multiple female interviewees revealed that whether or not a firm had women at all levels was important in determining if the firm welcomed and promoted women.

Women Are Less Likely Than Men to Consider Investing as a Career Path

A 2016 consulting firm report on women in financial services in thirty-two countries found that a majority of IM firms believe "the image of asset management firms may deter qualified women from applying, as may a lack of knowledge about the industry among graduates who have no specific reason to be interested in the topic."[11] Our research confirms this hypothesis. Male undergraduates are 58 percent more likely than women to consider a career in investment management and 50 percent more likely to choose a career in financial services.

Our survey of undergraduates found that exposure to someone who works in IM has the most influence on undergraduates' career choices. Women with family members in financial services are 1.6 times more likely to pursue a career in IM. Academic exposure to finance-related topics is also important in promoting female students' understanding of finance and IM. But it doesn't have to be a family member; it could also be a female finance professor, friends in the industry, a guest speaker, or even an article about a high-profile investor.

The two ends of the exposure spectrum came up in our primary research. An undergraduate student who was hired as an investment banking analyst on graduation credits much of her success to the influence of her (finance professional) mother. "My mom has always had a huge influence on me. It is really nice to see that your mom loves what she does. So, I think that is what got me interested in [finance]." Contrast this with another student, who told us, "I don't have someone close to me to expose me to finance." She initially chose an accounting major, yet once exposed to finance at college, added it as a second major.

If she is exposed to a high-profile female investor, a female undergraduate is 2.4 times more likely to consider entering the field. This exposure can be very limited—as brief as a guest lecture. One student attributed her interest in impact investing to hearing about the topic from a female guest speaker in class. "I got really interested in doing impact investing when the head of impact investing for a company came and spoke in my class. She had very similar experiences and interests as me, and I felt like I could relate to her a lot, and that's what inspired me to think, 'That's what I want to do in the future.' "

Friends in the industry are also influential in women's decisions to pursue a career in finance and investment management. "Finding people who I can engage with and relate to really strengthens my mindset of believing that I'm able to pursue that, or being certain that this is what I want to do."

Exposure within the classroom matters, too. Women who have taken a class with a female professor are 1.4 times more likely to understand careers and job titles in the investment management profession. As one student said,

> I've always been interested in finance. I think it definitely came down to thinking that I wasn't capable of it. But when I was connected with a female professor, I started to research finance more and realize that it's not all investment banking opportunities, and there are a lot of opportunities in finance that aren't as pressure focused.

Women Are Less Knowledgeable Than Men About the Industry and the Jobs Available to Them

In chapter 2 we provided an overview of the analyst and PM roles—in part because there is a dearth of readily accessible information about the IM career path and how to get yourself on it. When students evaluate professional options, they don't just need role models; they also need to understand the specific functions of each job as well as career paths. Based on our research, men are almost twice as likely as women to understand the specific careers and job titles available in IM.

Here's another perspective. When women hear that performance in IM is *quantifiable*, they pay attention.

> When I was trying to figure out what career path in finance to pursue, one of my female mentors shared an article with me that pointed out that as a portfolio manager, your performance results are like your "scorecard." So for women, there's less ambiguity and

possible unconscious bias when being compared to their male counterparts. That was incredibly eye-opening to me and a huge driver
as to why I decided to pursue investment management, and I never
would have learned it without my female mentor.

Women Are Less Confident Than Men in Their Ability to Land an IM Job

Earlier we talked about the importance of confidence in IM as a career,
and we will devote several pages to it in chapter 6. Confidence is also
important in the interviewing process. Many studies have shown that
women have lower levels of confidence than men. If you aren't confident that you have a chance of getting the job, that underconfidence
will shine through either in the interview or self-selection out of the
interview process entirely. Our survey found that male undergraduates
are 2.1 times more confident than female undergraduates that they
will find an IM job.

Fortunately, however, our survey found that confidence in a woman's ability to find a job in IM significantly improved with exposure to
other females in the industry. Women who knew a high-profile female
investor were twice as confident that they would be able to find a job
in IM than women who did not. Likewise, women who had friends in
the industry were twice as confident that they would be able to find a
job in IM than women who did not. As one student athlete explained,
"My coach has done a very good job at exposing us to successful
women in business. She does panels of successful women, and those
help us build the confidence that we need to go into whatever field we
want to, which in my case is business."

Exposure to financial literacy also had a positive impact on wom-
en's confidence in pursuing an IM career. Women who had taken
financial literacy classes were 20 percent more confident that they
would be able to find a job in IM than women who did not.

Conclusion: Understanding the Career and Exposure Are the Keys

Overall, undergraduate men are far more likely to consider IM careers than women. And as long as the industry is mostly "pale male," it will be difficult to lure talented undergrads outside this demographic—particularly since Gen Zers are more focused than prior generations on diversity. One student attributed her decision to accept a full-time offer to the company's efforts to improve diversity, even though she described her group as mostly white. Without specific diversity initiatives to make people like her feel included and supported, recruiting young women will continue to be difficult. We will provide some examples of these in our solutions section; for now, hold the thought that simply appearing to focus on diversity can help IM firms recruit entry-level women.

It's clear that the IM firms themselves must take on the bulk of the change to improve gender diversity. But there are also ways to enact change much earlier, before the start of young women's careers. Our constellation of female investors in chapter 8 is a veritable North Star for young women looking to enter the industry. And even if female undergraduates can't meet these women in person, we hope that these virtual role models will give women the conviction to say, "If she can do it, so can I."

5

Why Don't Women Choose Investing Careers?

The MBA Pipeline: Columbia Business School
as a Case Study

One of your authors is an adjunct professor at Columbia Business School (CBS), and it was her experience of teaching classes with 90 percent male students that got her interested in writing this book. Ellen has been teaching the same class (investing in the high-yield bond market) for eight years—and the gender demographics of the class have actually gotten worse. Recognizing that "data" is not the plural of "anecdote," we will nonetheless inform you that in the first year that Ellen taught the class, 17 percent of the students were women; in her most recent class, women made up only 8 percent. CBS's student body, meanwhile, is 40 percent female.[1] Ellen's (largely male) adjunct peers, as well as the administration, observe the same phenomenon and are as committed to changing this as she is. But how?

In this chapter we'll switch to Ellen's perspective as an adjunct professor of finance at CBS, one of the leading pipelines into IM. The anecdotes, gathered over an eight-year teaching career and supplemented by conversations with students and other CBS professors, seek to provide insights into the barriers that women face in pursuing IM careers once they reach the opposite end of the educational spectrum (see chapter 4, which featured undergraduate women at the beginning of their career exploration). After we review the roadmap toward an

IM internship and career, we will discuss the experience of one female MBA student and her journey to becoming an IM practitioner.

Setting the Stage: Inside Ellen's Classroom—High-Yield Bond Markets 101

I'm standing at the podium in a CBS classroom that seats sixty, which is filled a bit beyond capacity with students who have used a big slug of their academic "bidding points" to take my class on investing in high-yield bonds. The students filter in, chatting and joking with one another on the heels of Christmas break, wearing jeans, baseball caps, athleisure, and, occasionally, a suit and tie, indicating a job interview at some point during the day. They choose the seats they'll sit in for the duration of the class, place their name placards in the slots provided for this purpose, produce the obligatory (presumably, nonalcoholic) beverage container from their backpacks, plug in their laptops, and scan the room to see who else they might know.

I do a scan myself, the same one I've done for the eight years I've taught this class, not for students I know but for the women in their ranks. Predictably, I struggle to count a half dozen. I am, obviously, a woman myself—a diminutive woman at that. I don't have the presence you might associate with a business school professor—by which I mean that I don't think I intimidate people. My course evaluations regularly mention that I am good at explaining industry jargon, approachable, sometimes even funny, and willing to talk candidly about my investing mistakes (I've made a few . . .)—in other words, I should be the kind of professor female students would want if they are new to investing in general, and my asset class in particular. But eight years after that first Columbia class, I've learned to accept the reality, and inertia, of the gender imbalance of my students. Although the student body of CBS is around 40 percent women, women generally don't sign up for my classes, because they are geared toward people who are interested in pursuing investing careers.

Rather than "people," I might as well say "men."

The number of women settles at a predictable 10 percent by the time all the seats are filled. Based on prior experience, these women will likely undercontribute in class discussions. In fact, class discussions will probably be dominated by a handful of white men with experience in the subject matter—men who think they could teach some of the class content. These men will have valuable, thoughtful, relevant things to say, but their familiarity with the course content coming in can crowd out less experienced but no less thoughtful perspectives. CBS offers tools for its adjunct faculty to address this issue, yet I still struggle to improve the breadth of participation.

When I started teaching at CBS, I wanted to introduce students to the career I have loved—at times, been consumed by—since I was in their shoes twenty-plus years ago: investment management. Eight years on, I doubt that I have won over any IM converts. The students who take my classes mostly know they want to be investors—and the students who might dabble in my subject matter in a lower-stakes world than CBS often conclude, in their first few weeks of the MBA program, that their lack of investing experience has already disqualified them from finding one of the coveted, relatively small number of IM jobs. Most students who pursue MBAs are career changers, yet the deck is stacked against career changers who are looking for IM jobs. So, as usual, I call my class to order knowing that I will be preaching to a choir of investment disciples and thinking ruefully, "There's always next year."

A Note on Methodology: Why Devote an Entire Chapter to Columbia's MBA Program?

Although it's possible to get into IM as a college graduate and build your career, it's much more common to pursue an IM career after completing business school. We don't have data on the percentage of PMs with MBAs, but anecdotally we know that most of our peers have them, and most large investment managers recruit at the top ten MBA programs—so it's important to identify gendered themes in the MBA portion of the pipeline.

The headline statistic might suggest that this part of the IM supply chain is doing its part for diversity: MBA programs are pretty close to gender parity. The student bodies of the top ten U.S. MBA programs (as ranked by the *Financial Times* in 2020[2]) are, on average, 42 percent female. Yet clearly this is not translating into a similar number of female analysts at the IM firms who recruit from them. Why?

To answer this question, rather than take a broad-brush approach to MBA programs, as we did in the prior chapter, we decided to focus on CBS as a case study to illustrate some of the barriers that female MBAs face as they pursue IM careers. CBS is widely recognized as offering one of the best IM training programs. Its respected Value Investing (VI) Program is built around the investing principles first outlined by Columbia professors Benjamin Graham and David Dodd in their landmark 1934 book, *Securities Analysis*. Students in the VI Program, which requires a separate application toward the end of the first year of the MBA, largely focus on IM jobs, and its rigorous curriculum puts participants in prime position for getting them.

CBS's reputation as a feeder into IM *should* attract a disproportionate number of women by leveling the playing field. Women are hoop-jumpers; if they believe that a credential like the VI Program will give them a leg up in their job search, they'll pursue it. Yet the number of women in the VI Program, though better than in Ellen's classes, still lags the student body average. The 2019–2020 class was the most balanced yet—a quarter are women, up from 15 percent over the last couple of years. In this chapter, using data from a survey of the Columbia Student Investment Management Club (CSIMA) and primary research conducted by a CBS student, we'll explore the recruiting and classroom practices that might discourage women from pursuing IM jobs. We will also use her experience as a case study.

Recruiting Processes: Do They Discourage Women from Applying?

Both of your authors earned MBAs before we were hired into IM, but we got there in different ways. When Ellen was in the recruiting pipeline twenty-plus years ago, an MBA was viewed as a career changer's passport stamp. She came from a background of consulting, spent her first year interviewing for a summer job on the sell side, and managed to leverage the sell-side job offer at the end of the summer into an entry-level position at a buy-side firm. Katrina found her post-MBA job in IM through an ad on the CFA Institute's website in 2000, right after the dotcom bust.

Neither of these scenarios is likely to play out for a 2021 Columbia Business School graduate.

Ellen benefited from two things. The first: luck (note: this helps in investing as well). The second: the relative unpopularity of IM jobs circa 1999, her graduation year. Many of her classmates followed the siren song of the dotcom boom, and many went the banking and consulting routes. IM was viewed as a staid, boring career path. Entry-level salaries were lower than those for other careers (e.g., banking). Happily, the hours were lower as well.

Twenty years on, a select group of MBA students in premium programs has caught onto the secret Ellen stumbled on almost by accident: IM is a terrific career, with substantial financial upside, intellectual stimulation often lacking in cookie-cutter finance jobs like investment banking, and, in most cases, a reasonable quality of life relative to other careers. The popularity of this career is illustrated by the admission statistics of Columbia's VI Program; it has roughly twice as many applicants as there are available slots. Imagine getting into a prestigious, top-ten MBA program and being told you are not eligible for the curriculum you came to study. And on the demand side, big IM firms use leading business schools as a recruiting pipeline, with a more standardized process than existed when Ellen was recruiting, including an established summer internship pipeline, on-campus presence, and more.

Despite the proximity of CBS to Wall Street, a plethora of high-profile investors as guest speakers, practitioners who lecture, and the coveted VI Program, it is very difficult for a Columbia MBA student to get a job in IM out of business school. Columbia's 2018 employment report shows that 15 percent of students went into IM jobs, but the true number of students in direct investing roles is 5 percent. Compare this with the sell side (investment banking and sales, research, and trading), in which 13 percent of CBS grads were hired in 2018.

Another complicating factor for students seeking IM jobs is the passive share shift; not only are there hordes of MBAs competing for jobs, there are also many talented unemployed people who have been downsized. And there are only 20 or so large IM firms—a number that, as we write, continues to decline as firms consolidate to compete against their passive brethren. The math of this is harsh: there are simply more (very qualified) applicants for IM jobs than there are IM jobs, and the intensity of the recruiting process reflects this imbalance.

First-Year MBA Recruiting: Getting a Summer Internship

As we surmised from our undergraduate interviews, we also believe the lack of information about careers in IM at the graduate level is an impediment to MBA recruiting, considering that, as you will read next, students have to hit the ground running in the first few months of their MBA to get an IM job. One of your authors can attest to this; she was mentored by a running friend in IM, who encouraged her to pursue her MBA and a career as an analyst/PM. If not for this mentor, she likely would not have heard about this great career option, at which she has excelled—despite attending a university closer in proximity to Wall Street than CBS.

Other industry participants agree. A 2016 report on women in financial services in thirty countries found that a lack of knowledge about the industry among graduate students might deter women from pursuing IM careers.[3] In our survey of CSIMA members, men were 14 percent more likely to agree with the statement, "I understand the specific careers/job titles available in investing," than were women—and remember, this is a self-selected group of students who are already focused on the career. Men were also 18 percent more likely to agree with the statement, "I understand how to become a portfolio manager."

IM interviews are not just "getting to know you" exercises; they are also real-life tests of investing acumen. Despite the fact that students have less than a semester's worth of MBA coursework when they start interviewing, they are expected to produce a polished stock pitch, in some cases before they have taken their first investing course. The average CBS first-year student looking for a job in IM spends more than forty hours on her stock pitch, which creates a high barrier to entry for this recruiting path.

Over the fall months, large IM firms do on-campus introductory presentations and host networking events, during which, in theory, students can ask questions about the career path while, in practice, they network and attempt to get themselves on interview schedules. Students submit their résumés for interview slots by around Thanksgiving for interviews in January. Other students who are not as prepared this early in the recruitment process should not be disheartened—there is a second round of IM recruiting after the traditional firms have wrapped up their offers. The Career Management Center (CMC) calls this round of recruiting "enterprise," and it's populated by firms that are smaller and have less full-time job offer potential. Enterprise recruiting takes place from February until right before the summer, reflecting some firms' "just in time" approach to summer hiring. Hedge funds make up a big portion of this group; although some of these hedge funds pride themselves on unabashedly recruiting summer interns as cheap labor, some serious hedge funds offer career potential for aspiring IM professionals. Some students with prior IM experience purposely pursue the enterprise route as a way of exploring nontraditional IM and/or to build their résumés. These students have the option to step back onto the traditional track, and some do end up returning to their prior IM employers.

This is a terrific path for the subset of students—most of whom already have IM experience—who decide early on that they want to work for a small firm, but for other students it's a second choice (versus getting an offer from a large IM firm). One faculty member wonders whether enterprise recruiting poses a particular challenge for women:

> Part of the issue is the weird recruitment process. Outside the big firms, it's so nontraditional—it's a lot of small firms, and students have to leverage their networks. One of the easiest things you can do as an MBA is go to work in investment banking—the recruiting process is so structured—whereas so many people in IM have these "I was very lucky" recruiting stories. Most people end up getting a job through someone they know. Does that maybe play into the gender disparity?

The benefit of going to a smaller rather than a larger firm is the perception that you'll likely end up doing more "real work" (i.e., research) at a smaller firm. Students who summer at small IM firms are taking a risk; because the chance of receiving a full-time offer is significantly less than at a large firm, the student could be back in the internship pool during her second year. The silver lining: it's not hard to explain why you didn't get an offer, as opposed to the uncomfortable spin required if you fail to get an offer from a big firm that uses the summer internship as a screening mechanism for full-time job candidates.

Let's pause here, midway through the recruiting process, and make some observations.

- For all the talk of career changers, IM is very hard to penetrate with no industry experience. There are apocryphal stories about IM firms that hire so-called nontraditional candidates (e.g., journalists), but the majority of students looking for IM jobs enter with industry background, which provides them with investing lingo and an understanding of the types of jobs that are available. There simply isn't enough time for students to explore multiple career paths, given that the recruiting process begins so soon after they arrive on campus. As one of our interviewees put it, "Lots of career switchers worried about whether they can get into the industry." Another faculty member echoed this: "Women who might think 'This looks like an interesting career path' see all these talented people who really want to work in IM, so they don't pursue it. Only those who come in with a passion for it stick with it." Developing a passion for something takes longer than the few weeks students have to declare a career focus.

- First-year networking events can take on the feel of fraternity hazing events, although this is changing in the #metoo era. That came through in our survey; women were 18 percent more likely to agree with the statement, "Investing is a male-dominated and sexist industry in which it is difficult to succeed as a woman." One quote from our interviews sums this up nicely: "[IM firm] happy hours are full of guys wanting to talk about sports and drink whiskey and using crude language. Icebreakers are more male oriented and typically happen at a bar where the TV is showing sports." Some firms have begun offering interns access to female-only events, but gendered informational sessions are not a step toward equality; rather, they are a kind of "separate but equal" system.

- The summer internship is one of the surest ways into an IM career. If you don't spend your summer in IM, you'll be hard pressed to craft a good story about why you're suddenly keen on it after a summer in, say, consulting. For students who are attending graduate schools in close proximity to financial centers (i.e., New York and Boston), an in-semester internship is another opportunity to pursue an IM career. Although one of us balanced a full-time job while going to graduate school part-time, she acknowledges that balancing the two was demanding. (The other of us has no clue how her coauthor managed this.)

- Developing a stock pitch is time-consuming and risky—but it is the only way into a coveted IM job. It's entirely possible that all the time spent on a pitch comes to naught—time that could have been spent exploring other career paths. If we accept that women are more risk averse than men, it follows that, as one [male] student observed, some women start out on the IM recruiting path and switch to investment banking when they realize how much better the odds are of finding an investment banking job—and how many hours they will have to take away from studying and prepping for interviews in order to hone their pitches. The irony of this is that investment banking jobs are notoriously demanding, with eighty-hour work weeks the norm. Incidentally, your authors are not the only industry participants who question why this is one of the few jobs where you have to prove you can do the job before you have the job. At the risk of stealing our own thunder, we propose reshaping this part of recruiting in our solutions section.

- Students must be (or at least, sound) firmly committed to investing as a career during the interview process. The CMC encourages students to talk about any investing experience they have had—which runs right into another gender bias area: how parents talk to their kids about money. Parents are more likely to talk about investing and money matters with their sons than with their daughters, which puts women at a disadvantage when it comes to memorable "I've always wanted to be an investor" stories. Having interviewed MBA candidates for her prior firm, Ellen can recall the earnest twenty-seven-year-old talking about how his investment banker dad gave him $10 to buy Mattel stock when he identified the growth potential of its Hot Wheels franchise at the age of five.

- The recruiting process lionizes actual investing to a fault. As one interviewee told us, "I often heard comments in interviews such as 'so you've never picked stocks before,' and even 'so you don't have any investing experience.' " It should go without saying that students in certain demographics are more likely to have grown up with parents who suggest they should "invest in what they know," à la Warren Buffett, not to mention those in demographics with the type of family wealth that permits investing at all. As one of our interviewees said, "I've been encouraged by mentors to start investing my own money; that's the only way to practice." What if you don't have any money?

- If experience isn't the best gauge of talent, then what is? One of our interviewees said, "In a few instances where I was given a mini case study on the spot about a new company or new industry, I did well. While prior experience can help in those situations, it's not necessary because a creative and critical thinker can also come up with satisfying answers or new angles." After two decades of actively investing, we concur with this statement. The best investors are indeed creative and critical thinkers who spot things the market doesn't—and that ability doesn't always correlate to the number of hours you spent on your pitch. Yet time and again, IM firms fall for the recruit who speaks their language. It doesn't take much time to learn jargon like "P/E ratio" and "debt to EBITDA." It's a lot harder in an interview to measure a candidate's potential to analyze, forecast, and interpret the numbers behind these and other terms.

A composite quote from our interviews sums up these barriers well: "Women without experience find it easy to be discouraged. Men tend to have greater confidence; they think they will be able to make the switch [into IM]."

Second-Year MBA Recruiting: Getting a Full-Time Job

For some fortunate MBAs, the summer job leads to a full-time offer. This is a win-win: the intern gets to know the company and is saved the time-consuming work of second-year recruiting. In exchange, the firm gets to know the intern through a ten-week interview process that culminates in a research project that showcases the intern's analytical skills.

Many students come out of their summer internships with no offer, either because things don't work out (this is by design, as the summer programs are meant to winnow the field of talented candidates) or because they were never meant to work out (at firms that see summer interns as cheap labor but do not have full-time positions available). All the work involved in the summer intern recruiting process is, retrospectively, a dress rehearsal for post-MBA recruiting. There is another stock pitch, a résumé update with the summer job details, and interview prep that includes a well-rehearsed rationale for the lack of a summer offer.

Can the Classroom Help Women MBAs Who Are Considering IM by Providing Female Role Models?

You will recall from the prior chapter that undergraduate women are more likely to consider IM when they know (even if in a very peripheral sense—know, or know of) women in the industry or have female finance professors. One of Columbia's big advantages for IM job seekers is its proximity to Wall Street, which makes it easy to lure talented practitioners into the classroom. CBS's Heilbrunn Center houses the school's large network of adjunct professors (including Ellen), who in turn draw in lots of practitioner guest lecturers (including Katrina). Perhaps not surprisingly, only 15 percent of the Heilbrunn Center faculty are female, compared with 21 percent of CBS's faculty as a whole.[4]

CBS students don't have the opportunity to take many classes with female finance professors, which limits one important source of role models for women MBAs. *The New York Times* published an in-depth exposé on female MBA students and faculty at Harvard Business School (HBS) in 2013.[5] Although it reads a bit sensationally, the overall themes of the piece—that female students are out-talked in the classroom and that female faculty are hazed by male students— are not limited to HBS. Ellen's classes are dominated by questions from male students; although fortunately she hasn't experienced the hazing described in the article, she has noticed that women stay quiet in class, even though participation is 15 to 20 percent of their final grade. We heard corroborating viewpoints in our interviews:

> Class participation skews toward males, but I don't feel females are uncomfortable. However, when the teacher makes male jokes, that leaves the females out a lot of times. As to class participation, women are self-conscious; they always feel they are not ready yet.

> Guys just blurt out things even if they are not completely sure. It would be nice to have more female investing professors.

Other faculty have observed this phenomenon as well. As one told us, "Males tend to be more vocal in my class; they are more likely to be overconfident or more decisive. This could appear as a good characteristic in interviews, but overconfidence can be a detriment to good results."

It's notable that one investing professor at CBS whose classes have consistently had higher numbers of women incorporates many female guest speakers into his curriculum. As he told us, "I bring back several former female students as guest lecturers each semester. I got kind of lucky with this—I had a few talented women early on in my teaching, so I have a Rolodex of female guest speakers now." It doesn't hurt that he goes out of his way to set a culture that is, well, nice—a safe space for students to pitch their ideas with constructive feedback, rather than an environment in which their classmates attack their reasoning and analysis.

Although having more female role models in the classroom—as either professors or guest lecturers—can only help, we believe that the recruiting practices discussed earlier are more detrimental to women's pursuit of IM jobs than anything that does or doesn't take place in the classroom. The good news is that this is potentially one of the easier things to change, as we discuss in our solutions section.

A Real-Life Female MBA's Story

To see what it takes to find an IM job, let's follow Columbia MBA student Tina through her recruiting journey. (Tina is a pseudonym; although she was happy to speak openly with us, she was more comfortable doing so anonymously.)

Tina viewed herself as a career changer, though she had quite a bit of industry experience. She started in public accounting, then went into endowment investing, where most recently she was a capital allocator at a multifamily office. Capital allocators are one step removed from portfolio managers; they select IM firms and portfolio managers for various asset classes. (You will meet some allocators and hear more about their role in the IM supply chain in chapter 12.) In her pre-MBA role, Tina made decisions about how much her firm should invest in various asset classes (stocks, bonds, etc.) and then chose managers for each asset class based on their track record and investing style. It might seem counterintuitive that the allocators lust after the jobs of portfolio managers, but the latter career is both more intellectually stimulating and more lucrative. The allocators are sometimes viewed as box-checkers, making sure that the strategies they select adhere to various quantitative and qualitative metrics. Yet they do reside in the big tent of IM, which gave Tina a bit of a leg up during the recruiting process.

Tina went to CBS in large part to make the transition from allocator to investor and was prepared for the rigor of the recruiting process.

As we mentioned earlier, this begins in October for first-year students, which gives incoming students a brief few weeks to explore career options. The compressed time frame means that most IM job seekers are like Tina: they have already decided on IM. In her own words,

> I am passionate about the IM industry because I think stock research is intellectually stimulating and fascinating. I love reading and learning about companies and making predictions about the future; I love numbers. I am also drawn to the industry because this job is meritocracy based and can give me a lot of autonomy and ultimately financial independence and freedom.

In other words, Tina didn't buy into some of the outsider myths about the industry; she understood its merits, and she knew which job she wanted.

For her stock pitch, Tina took the CMC's advice to "follow your passion" and chose a beauty company. As noted earlier, an aspiring MBA will spend forty-plus hours developing her pitch—hours that she stole from her coursework. With all the other demands on her time, Tina admitted, "I struggled with setting aside time to develop pitches and putting my ideas down on paper." She took advantage of several resources available to CBS first-year students, including the Women in Investing (WIN) conference at Cornell (a program we will discuss in more detail in section III), where students give their pitches and are critiqued by a large group of seasoned female investors. Students can also get feedback on their pitches from second-year students affiliated with the student IM club (CSIMA), industry alum volunteers, panels of judges organized by the Investment Ideas Club, coaches and fellows provided by the CMC, and an online service called Wall Street Prep.

Tina returned from Christmas break with a refined stock pitch and a full slate of interviews. During the recruiting process, it became clear to her that "unless the recruiting company is highly open minded and deliberate about hiring career switchers, it is extremely difficult for career switchers to outshine nonswitchers throughout the whole process." She found that despite CMC statements to the contrary, "in general, most interviewers are still more interested in the stocks I looked at [i.e., her prior investing experience] than in me as a person."

Despite these challenges, Tina emerged from first-year recruiting with four job offers—an excellent result that's indicative of her attractiveness as a candidate. She ultimately decided to go to a large investment manager. Tina was qualified, hard working, and well prepared. She didn't get a full-time offer from her summer employer, but her experience there helped her land a full-time offer from another prestigious IM firm during second-year recruiting.

In case we didn't make this clear before, Tina, our CBS career changer, is a superstar. She is all that an MBA usually is—smart, hardworking, motivated—as well as fun to be around, thoughtful, and creative. That's why we think her words are the best way to close this chapter, as they summarize a number of its themes.

I know investing is a very hard and stressful job. Data has shown that most active funds underperform the market. The industry is highly competitive and is facing lots of structural headwinds. Many believe the industry will continue to shrink. Additionally, your results are marked-to-market every day. From my conversations with various analysts, portfolio managers, and their families, I kept hearing things like "Don't get into the industry," "It's super stressful," "If you find out in five years you are not good at stock picking, you'll be done and no one will hire you," and "If your stock works, the portfolio manager takes most of the credit, and if it doesn't, you are the one to blame." I also know temperament plays a big part in investing. So sometimes I wonder, am I well suited to pursue a successful career in IM? Would I fail miserably even if I work very hard?

We applaud Tina's determination to work in IM, and we know that she will do great despite the laundry list of concerns that others voiced about her decision to pursue a career in the investment field.

Now that Tina is set to start her career as an investment analyst, we'll move to the next part of the pipeline—inside IM firms like the one that hired her. Unfortunately, the quotes embedded in Tina's comments have some merit, and she is right to gird herself for a tough slog. Female attrition rates in an IM career are higher than those of their male counterparts.[6] Our next chapter looks at why the industry fails to retain and promote women.

6

Looking Inside Investment Management

Identifying Barriers to Women's Advancement

The last two chapters provided the perspectives of women who haven't worked in IM, apart from Tina's short stint as a summer intern. In this chapter we're moving into the lion's den to introduce you to some of the barriers that women face once they're hired into this male-dominated industry.

Chances are that you've read a lot of the same studies we have about gender dynamics in the workplace. If so, a lot of what you'll read in this chapter will sound familiar—and that is exactly the message we want to convey. The cultural and structural barriers that women face in many, if not most, workplaces are amplified by some of the characteristics of IM. After all our research, we've come to view our industry as ground zero for the gender diversity debate.

This book isn't meant to include an exhaustive list of studies about gender inequality in the workplace; rather, we've provided a compilation of the ones we found particularly relevant to IM. We've already shared our view that this is not a #metoo issue of ass-grabbing and "sleep with me or you're fired" behavior. We did not hear any stories of overt sexual harassment in our interviews, and although that doesn't mean it doesn't happen, many women we spoke with shared stories about positive male mentors who had helped, not hurt, their careers.

The lack of #metoo backlash makes the dearth of women all the more confounding, but this absence of overt barriers to gender balance in IM must not translate into a barrier to solutions to IM's homogeneity.

This is not an exhaustive list, but we've distilled our view of why it's so hard for women to succeed in IM into seven themes, some of which intersect.

1. Confidence
2. Risk
3. Ambition
4. Low-value seats
5. Networking and politicking
6. The promotion delay
7. Stay-at-home-wife (SAHW) syndrome

We'll explore these themes using data from studies and breathe life into them with the voices of women we've interviewed. One caveat: we aren't going to talk about work–life balance in this chapter, because we've reserved an entire chapter for that important topic.

Confidence: Why Is There No Such Thing as a "Con Woman"?

We've been making oblique references to the role of confidence in IM from the prologue up to now. This is where we get explicit. *Confidence is integral to success in IM.* Its importance runs through every part of the supply chain and lifecycle of a successful PM.

- When MBAs interview for IM jobs, they have to project confidence in their stock pitch. (The standard intro is, "I believe this stock has 40 percent upside in the next year.")
- When analysts pitch their ideas to PMs, they have to project confidence. (A standard question from PMs is, "What's your level of conviction in this?")

- When analysts transition to PMs, they have to project confidence. (The standard pitch to management is, "My recommendations have outperformed the peer group by 20 percent.")
- When PMs pitch their services to clients, they have to project confidence. (The standard question from clients is, "How will you outperform the market?")

Higher-than-average confidence is a prerequisite for a successful investing career for two reasons. First, the notion that you can beat the market goes against what you learn in Investing 101: that markets are efficient. Saying you can beat a benchmark is by definition a statement that you're smarter than most investors.

Second, investing requires being wrong sometimes—and it takes a higher-than-average degree of confidence to watch the market turn against you. Don't just take it from us; here are some quotes about how it feels to be wrong.

I can't tell you how many times I wanted to stop and just throw in the towel and be like, forget it.

You can't look to either other investors or the market to pat you on the back and signal you're doing the right thing.

It takes a pretty specific personality type to succeed as a woman in IM; you have to project confidence. Women suffer a greater penalty for lack of confidence than men.

If you need that pat on the back to feel like you're doing a good job, this is not the career for you because the market will just kick you around. You have to just stick with it and be willing to stand alone.

Our way of seeing the world is, if I work hard, things are going to turn out right. But in money management, you have to be prepared to work hard and things don't turn out the way you expect.

Everybody has to have resilience and stamina to say, "well, I'm going to take this pain. I'm going to review what happened and learn the lessons." If you ask me, "Why don't women stay in asset management?" I think it's how hard it is to stand up after that stumble.

Men and women are distinctly unequal when it comes to confidence.[1] Men's innately higher degree of confidence gives them a leg up in a career that demands it at higher-than-average levels. Incidentally, there is no correlation between confidence and competence; in fact, overconfidence, which is difficult to distinguish from confidence, can be antithetical to good investment results. Again, we'll let some of our peers speak for themselves.

The conviction-to-analysis ratio is higher for men, and that's not a good thing, although it can lead to career success.

Compared with my male counterparts, I was always proving something. The men believed they were good stock pickers and they could do this.

I noticed early on that the guys who were banging their desks and yelling the loudest were being heard—the ones who expressed a confidence level that made you think they'd done all their work and couldn't be wrong.

I was less confident and more timid, and my [male] colleagues were louder and more convincing.

Even confident women learn early on to tone it down, because exhibitions of confidence are viewed differently in men and women. A *New Yorker* article entitled "Lean Out—The Dangers for Women Who Negotiate" makes the case, based on multiple studies, that "our implicit gender perceptions mean that the advice that women stand up for themselves and assert their position strongly . . . may not have the intended effect. It may even backfire." Worse, studies show that "female leaders who try to act in ways typically associated with male leaders—assertive, authoritative, directive [we would add "confident" to this list]—are seen far more negatively than males."[2]

This insidious bias against women acting like men—in many cases, this meant acting confident—came up over and over again in our interviews. A male interviewee summed it up well: "Women who don't suffer fools gladly are much less likely to be accommodated than men. A woman can be 60 percent as offensive as a man, but she will get voted off the island and he won't."

There's an analogue to the con woman concept: Peter (as in the Peter Principle) is a man. Howard Marks, the cochairman and cofounder of Oaktree, told us,

> One of our greatest mistakes in Oaktree's early years consisted of being too patient with underperformers. Ironically, those under-performers generally weren't women, since due to biases in society, among other things, women had a lower probability of being pro-moted to positions from which they would underperform.

We suggest that women's confidence deficit is somewhat to blame for their inability to "Peter Principle" their way into PM roles.

Risk: We Can Take It—We Just Don't Talk About It the Same Way Men Do

Risk-taking, like confidence, is viewed as an essential element of investing acumen. Similarly, there's a fine line between good, per-formance-enhancing risk-taking and bad, "swinging for the fences" risk-taking. And, like confidence, risk-taking behavior can manifest differently in men and women—although the evidence on this is mixed. Some studies show that women investors make fewer risky financial decisions than men. For example, the global BlackRock Investor Pulse survey[3] found that 72 percent of women as opposed to 59 percent of men rejected investments in riskier equities, bonds, or real estate. On the other hand, an intriguing 2018 study that tracked 20,000 mutual fund managers over two decades found that both women and men took more risk when they worked with a higher proportion of female fund manager colleagues. The study's authors speculate that this is attributable to a so-called safe haven effect. In other words, if women are (at least perceived to be) less risk-taking than men, their team-mates (whether male or female) think it's acceptable to take more risk because someone is making up for it on the other side.[4] Lest you think it was just the men acting this way, this tendency to take more risk was even more common among the women in the study—which suggests that women fund managers are even more likely than men to assume their "sistren" won't take a lot of investing risk.

But even if women do take less risk than men, does this correlate with lower returns? One intriguing take on this comes from Malcolm Gladwell. His 2010 *New Yorker* article about the myth of the high-risk entrepreneur lays out his thesis: "The truly successful business-man [authors' note: or investor!] is anything but a risk-taker. He is a predator, and predators seek to incur the least risk possible while hunting." Successful people, whether founders or investors, don't take excessive, aggressive risk; rather, they take limited, calculated risk based on analysis.

The cult of the risk-taking entrepreneur, or investor, is a myth, according to Gladwell. "Would we so revere risk-taking if we realized that the people who are supposedly taking bold risks in the cause of entrepreneurship are actually doing no such thing?" Gladwell won-ders. His description of John Paulson, the subprime superstar from *The Big Short*, illustrates how successful risk-taking works in IM. Paulson is the antithesis of a bravado male analyst discussing his ten-bagger pitch. Rather, he is a razor-sharp research analyst whose approach to risk sounds more like that of some of the women we interviewed than of Leonardo DiCaprio's character in *The Wolf of Wall Street*.[5]

Gladwell's research helps to illustrate how images of what risk-taking should look like do not match up with good results. Despite the lack of correlation between risk-taking and results in real life, many people in IM hold firmly to the belief that good results require a strong risk appetite. If you believe this, you are more likely to hire, and listen to, men than women, because women don't verbalize their risk appetite as much as men do.

So, what do the women in our industry think about risk-taking? There are a number of perspectives on this, ranging from…

> It would be great for women to play to win rather than playing not to lose. Some women are so risk-averse that they hedge away all the upside—I've seen that a lot. We just need to take the bet.

. . . to

> The risk aversion thing [i.e., the idea that women are more risk-averse than men] is a myth.

And we refer you to the article cited earlier: women perceive *each other* to be lower-risk investors.

We've worked with plenty of women who are sharp, calculated risk-takers, à la Paulson, but we've also noted what many of our interviewees mentioned: women and men *talk* about risk differently. It's not that women are more risk-averse—it's that they're more risk-aware. Sometimes that's because they've done more diligent work than their male peers, which means it's harder to overlook the downside case.

And that is not necessarily a bad thing for investing. From the perspective of successful portfolio managers,

> I do notice that women present their case and include the "cons," while men just present the case. Women look at risk-reward more holistically; men have more of a tendency to go with "pros" and get caught up in momentum trades.

Women should actually be better at this job than men. They're much more likely to do their research and less likely to get sucked into a momentum trade, like bitcoin. [Note: this comment is from a male.]

Women use a different vocabulary—not wrong, just different. And women are more process oriented than men, although they get to the same outcomes. When you're more process oriented, it can be hard to distinguish between that and excessive risk aversion. [Note: this comment is from a male.]

Men and women express conviction differently. When women give ideas, they give the other side, which is a very talented approach to investing. Women don't have less conviction; they just express it differently.

Ah, *conviction*—a close cousin to confidence, which we discussed earlier. Although perceptions of risk-taking and confidence sometimes intermingle, both are crucial in investing, and it's difficult to differentiate between good and bad manifestations of them. This can be a challenge to women if they are perceived to be less capable in either respect. If there is any difference in risk-taking between men and women, based on our interviews and personal observation, we believe that it is women's greater willingness to weigh both sides of a recommendation—"not only the upside but the downside," as one of our interviewees put it. This can come across as a lack of conviction, but it strikes us as good discipline, as two PMs who have managed money through market ups and downs (including the global financial crisis of 2008 and, as we write, the unfolding COVID-19 pandemic).

The perception of higher female risk aversion has implications outside investing. If you want to become a PM, you don't just have to take market risk—you also have to take career risk. Research shows that we are not as good at this as men are.[6] In chapter 2, we talked about how transitioning to PM requires self-promotion, lobbying, and calculated positioning. We heard from senior people in charge of hiring and promotion that women's more conservative approach to career advancement sometimes comes across as hesitation to take on the "next" role (e.g., PM)—when in fact, it's better described as a more measured approach. A representative quote:

> We set up training for women to ask for their next career move. Our facilitator called on every single woman to speak—I realized I hadn't heard a lot them speak! Just giving women tools so they know how to raise their hands helps. The facilitator told them, These are just normal things you shouldn't be embarrassed to do [e.g., self-promotion]. Early on in their careers, women progress because they're focused and good at their jobs. Men seem to be more adept at that midpoint where it's not just the work you do but also the self-promotion that gets you to the next level. Many times when you tell women versus men we're thinking about you for this role, men say yes, but women ask questions, which is perceived as no. As a management team, we continued the conversation when women asked questions; we didn't view it as a no. We stopped thinking of hesitation as a no.—retired female investment management CEO

All organizations looking to improve gender diversity, particularly within management ranks, should take these learnings to heart. Asking questions does not mean no. We know from studies, interviews, and our own experience that women tend to overprepare, and questioning should be seen in this light. We're asking questions not because we're disinterested in the position but because we want to understand the position better. No, of course, means no. Asking a question does not.

Female Ambition: Damn Unpretty

According to a McKinsey/Lean In study, "Women in entry-level roles in financial services seldom envision themselves in a top executive position; only 26 percent aim for this goal, as compared to 40 percent of their male peers and 31 percent of entry-level women across all industries."[7] We think the PM role falls into the "top executive position" category. As discussed in chapter 2, you often have to self-promote into the PM role—being a good analyst isn't enough. Unfortunately, research shows that women have developed strategies for masking their gender in response to the biases they face in the workplace, including *intentional invisibility*, a "set of risk-averse, conflict-avoidant strategies that women professionals . . . employ to feel authentic, manage competing expectations in the office, and balance work and familial responsibility."[8] Women are deliberately hiding in work environments with biased expectations to avoid backlash. The problem is that you can't hide if you want to transition from analyst to PM; the loudest voices are often the ones whom management views as ready for the role, because part of the role involves expressing your views in public. If women are hiding, putting their heads down, being good worker bees rather than the people talking the loudest at the weekly investment call, they're not positioning themselves for a PM role. In fact, they may not even be positioning themselves for the best analyst roles—our next point.

Low Value Seats: Women's Work in IM

Tanya was a brilliant, focused, newly-minted MBA from a top-five school when she joined a large fund manager. She was assigned a superstar female mentor as she started her analyst career covering a small, unloved sector. Tanya unexpectedly found herself pregnant a few months after she began her job, and she never crawled out of this hole. The industries she inherited after her first one were as dull as dishwater; she was the analyst serving Brussel Sprouts (regulated utilities) to the PMs, alongside analysts who got to serve flourless chocolate cake (tech). She delayed having a second child so that she could diligently work her way into a better analytical place, and she did comprehensive, thoughtful analysis of all of her industries, with consistently good recommendations that deftly straddled the risk/return divide. Tanya served lemonade alongside her Brussel Sprouts, even finding ways to make money in out-of-favor industries.

In our opinion, this investment acumen should have been what senior management was looking for as they planned for PM succession—but Tanya knew that she needed to build her own case for a transition from analyst to PM. She started mentioning her desire to make this move at every semi-annual review, and brought along numbers to show how well her recommendations performed relative to other companies in the same industries. Year after year, Tanya lobbied quietly for herself. Finally, after being overlooked for promotion to PM multiple times, she threw in the towel.

We tell this composite story here to demonstrate the lifetime damage that low value seats can inflict on women who don't self-advocate early or often enough. Research across multiple industries suggests that women are more likely to be placed in low-profile, low-potential jobs. In IM, "low-profile" can relate to industry coverage at the analyst level. While data is hard to come by, according to *Institutional Investor's* report "Where Are All the Women?", female analysts score highly in beverages and household products, department stores and biotech. A study of sell-side analyst participation in earnings call Q&A showed a marked skew towards women in consumer discretionary and consumer staple sectors (16 percent and 19 percent of the analyst population, respectively) versus IT (8 percent).[9] Why do we say these are low value sectors? Over the past 10 years, the S&P has returned 187 percent, vs Consumer Staples 133 percent—and IT, 330 percent. (As a side note, retail was one of your authors' first industries.)[10]

The low-value seat effect also takes place at the PM level. You might recall reading about this in chapter 3; some of our interviewees spoke of choosing a less desirable asset class (for example, small cap, fixed income, ESG) in order to get a PM spot. Over several decades in IM, women have sometimes found success taking the jobs that men didn't want. In some cases, they have been rewarded for taking less desirable jobs, as some of these sectors ended up being more "alpha-rich" (that is, easier to beat the index) than high-profile ones like large-cap U.S. stocks. However, these weren't "good" portfolios to manage when women originally took them on—and now that the industry is waking up to the potential for alpha generation, some men are attempting to muscle in on what used to be classified as women's work.

A corollary to this is that ambitious, high-performing women are sometimes afraid to say no—because they fear not being asked again. Howard Marks, co-chairman and co-founder of Oaktree, told us, "One of my mentees, a woman, has worked her way into increasingly senior jobs. She has always taken the increasingly important jobs she was offered, to the point where I had to tell her that she needed to be more selective or else she would become overloaded. Women are sometimes afraid to say no because, first, they want to show what they can do, and second, they may be afraid they'll get only so many chances." One of us found herself ruefully nodding at Howard's comments; I was dubbed "the girl who can't say no" because I took on *everything* early in my career, from mediocre industry coverage to my first PM role in the firm's struggling institutional business (versus the higher-profile, bigger AUM fund side of the company) to responsibility for organizing the firm's biannual conference.

Networking and Politicking

Office politics—that is, the ability to manage both the work itself and an office's social environment—is a key aspect of moving up the corporate ladder. Networking barriers are faced by *any* salient minority in a corporate workplace, not only women. "After one gets the initial job, social skills separate the wheat from the chaff in high finance," according to a managing partner at a New York–based private equity fund.[11] If you've ever worked for anyone other than yourself, you know that whether you've got 10, 100, or thousands of co-workers, the traits that lead to success in office politics are complex and nuanced. Ben Dattner, a New York–based business consultant, believes that one of the keys to successfully navigating office politics is "mastering personal relationships at multiple levels."[12]

But investing is all about your *quantifiable* performance relative to a benchmark, right? Many people, including us, entered IM because we thought it offered a quantifiable, fair performance gauge. But because we naively over-emphasize results at the expense of networks, "Women chronically underinvest in networking. Being excellent at what you do is a prerequisite for success, but not enough," according to Katie Koch, head of Goldman Sachs Asset Management. Another quote from a successful female PM, who feels she succeeded *despite* her lack of politicking, sums up the attitudes of many of our interviewees: "I was always horrible at networking and finding advocates—I was just good at my job." One interviewee, echoing others, found that: "When I look back, I was often puzzled by who was anointed, and why." If you're thinking a woman who retired herself early from a hostile hedge fund environment fed us that quote, guess again—it's from Paul Haaga, the retired *male* chairman of a top-ten fund management company. A successful [male] PM, retired hedge fund manager Whitney Tilson, put it this way: "One woman who'd spent her career on Wall Street told me: 'Women tend to build relationships with other women based on who'll be great bridesmaids at their wedding. Men are more likely to build relationships with those who'll help their careers.' "

Author Megan Tobias Neely corroborates this in her seminal paper about how patrimonialism leads to inequality in the hedge fund industry. Hedge fund managers skew even more white male than traditional investment managers. Given that the profession has a high degree of uncertainty (recall that one of the most famous books on investing is titled *A Random Walk Down Wall Street*[13]), a system of patronage—that is, networks of people who look and think like they do—has sprung up to protect hedge fund managers who find themselves taking the wrong fork on their walks. As one [male] hedge fund manager put it, "We go on ski trips and have poker nights—it would just be weird to have a 25-year-old, single woman on these trips—she'd be a fish out of water. There's just not enough critical mass for women to feel comfortable in these settings. And it's uncomfortable for the guys too."

We are not blaming the men—quite the contrary. We have seen these patriarchal networks in action with good results, for example, the Tiger Fund seeding the Tiger Cubs. While our "Money Manifesto" at the book's end sets lofty diversity goals for our industry, we don't think there's any value in attacking this patriarchal structure—because the results should speak for themselves. If the rest of the industry takes up our challenge, and we see a meaningful increase in women investors rather than a salient, token minority of them, the benefits of gender-diverse teams will shine through. Once these diverse teams beat homogenous hedge funds, the latter (as both investors and business managers) will see what the literature has been showing us for decades—diverse teams outperform.[14]

Of course, it's easiest to network with people who are similar to you—but with so few female PMs and low female representation in IM generally, this is a career-limiting view of networking. While this is by no means universally true, based on our own anecdotes and experience, often the women who make it to the top do so by "behaving more like the guys," as one interviewee said she'd been advised to do. While not becoming a golf course regular, she found it easier to "be one of the guys" by enjoying expensive port and Cuban cigars at the end of a long work dinner. For one of your authors, who has been pregnant four times, the limitations of these "networking" events are clear. And it's not just the nine months when the child is in utero, it's the pre-months of "trying" and the postpartum months of breast-feeding.

And here's the crux of the problem of inadequate networks in IM (and hence why having a diverse professional network is so important): Being wrong—that is, putting up bad numbers periodically—is part of the job—but it can be hard to tell if someone is wrong in a good (contrarian who will be proved right) way or a more permanent (bad investor) way. As one of our interviewees put it, "Women have no natural advocates in the room when this kind of thing [underper-formance] happens. When a PM hits a rough patch, guys are much more likely to get 'oh, he's just going through a rough patch' than women." Networking builds political capital for investing's inevita-ble rough patches. Retired hedge fund manager Whitney Tilson told us, "During the 2008–2009 financial crisis, women and men were laid off in droves. In the aftermath, however, one woman friend of mine observed that the men got hired back more quickly because their golfing buddies looked out for them." Having more SoulCycle sisters looking out for women will help once we achieve gender parity; until that point, we need to develop diverse professional networks.

A word on women-only events, which are becoming more preva-lent in our industry (as well as other male-dominated ones). We sup-port these (and in fact, we've attended many ourselves). We believe that until we hit the 30 percent mark, in which we transition from a salient minority to a relevant one, these will be vital to helping achieve gender parity. But our ultimate goal is to wean ourselves off these events—for them to achieve planned obsolescence. We want a world in which women-only events will look as anachronistic as business meetings held at strip clubs.

There's another angle on this issue: the corporate C-suite, where women are underrepresented. Only 20 percent of C-Suite positions are held by women,[15] which understates the imbalance, as women in the C-suite are less likely to have roles that lead to the CEO position. Only ~5 percent of CEOs and 15 percent of CFOs are women, while an ISS study found that 44 percent of women in the C-Suite are in Human Resources, 19 percent are General Counsel, and 17 percent are the Chief Administrative Officer. Corporations, like the IM firms that allocate capital to them, give women "soft" roles.[16]

This matters for women investors because in addition to relation-ships with their co-workers, they need to cultivate relationships with the management teams of the companies in their portfolios. Every investment conference at a resort features a slate of tee-times which match CEOs and CFOs with investors (ever so kindly facilitated by investment bankers). Women face the same networking requirements, and hurdles, in this peer group as they do in the office. As long as the C-Suite—in particular, the CEO and CFO roles—is gender-imbalanced, bonding activities in which important information might be conveyed will skew male. This information doesn't have to rise to the level of inside information to be relevant; it can be as simple as reading body language in response to a pointed question with a "can't comment" answer. Access to management, whatever its backdrop, can be critical to good investment decisions.

At the risk of stating the obvious, we will duly cite a CalSTRS's study of "Attitudes Towards Diversity in the Investment Management Industry" which found that 66 percent of the women and minorities surveyed believed that being a woman or minority had hindered their investment management career.[17] While this quote could go anywhere in the book, we highlight it here because it is directly related to the networking/politicking theme. If you don't work with many people who look like you, it's a lot harder to network your way into plum PM roles, and to politic your way through periods of bad numbers.

The Promotion Delay

Hopefully you remember our discussion of PM compensation from chapter 2. To recap, a potentially large part of a PM's compensation comes from a bonus tied to outperformance relative to a benchmark. But that's not all that the track record is used for; it's truly the heart and soul of a PM's resume. When you go to interview for another PM job, the first thing you'll be asked for is your results. And when you live and die by your track record, the longer it is the better you are perceived to be. One of the firms we have worked for doesn't pay much attention to any PM's results if they go back less than four years. We're sympathetic to this view; as investment analysts, we need at least four years of results from the companies we research, too!

This is a problem for women because they wait longer to be "promoted" (in IM, from analyst to PM) than men do. In a *60 Minutes* interview, the CEO of Salesforce and the former CEO of Dupont talked about the promotion delay, i.e., the tendency for men to be promoted with shorter tenure than women: "We were promoting women every 30 to 36 months into the same kind of jobs as we were promoting men every 18 to 24 months."[18] While the promotion delay hurts women in many industries, its impact is particularly acute in investing—because the most important part of your resume is the investing track record you've built.

This is echoed by industry research. A study of the career outcomes of mutual fund managers found that "all else equal, female fund managers are less likely to be promoted and have shorter tenures than male managers"—and that this finding was more relevant to women who were part of a portfolio management team.[19] In other words, working in teams hurts a woman's career prospects. The study also found that women have worse career trajectories than male managers in similar circumstances, even after controlling for performance and for their differing fund management responsibilities. (So much for the benefits of being a team player.)

SAHW Syndrome: It's a Thing

> It always seemed like our male colleagues were benchmarking us against their wives.
>
> —SUCCESSFUL FEMALE PM

> I heard "happy wife, happy life" in every meeting we did.
>
> —SUCCESSFUL FEMALE PM

A heterosexual man with a stay-at-home-wife (we're calling her a SAHW) is more likely to have a negative attitude toward working women.[20] Since a CFA Institute study found that 79 percent of women in IM have a spouse with a full-time occupation, versus 51 percent of men, that means half of our male peers are potentially suffering from this negative attitude.[21] Authors Barber, Scherbina, and Schlusche take this one step further and suggest that since finance is one of the highest-paying fields, men in the industry are more likely to have a SAHW and, thus, this negative attitude about their female colleagues than men in other lower-paying careers.[22] That's not bringing your work home, that's bringing your home to work! Even more disconcertingly for those of us who work alongside men with SAHWs, research shows that men are likely to resent wives who make more than they do— which likely doesn't translate into warm, fuzzy feelings about their high-earning female co-workers.[23]

Selling Women Short shows that norms regarding the cultural division of labor within the household are transferred to the workplace.[24] Since half of our male co-workers have SAHWs, it's inevitable that the stereotypical attitudes of the role of the husband breadwinner/ wife homemaker creep into meetings and management decisions. Yes, we have all heard the stories about the female CEO who was asked in a meeting to make coffee—before the guy who asked realized who she was. Happily, this appears to be changing; anecdotally, we have seen a shift from laying bets as to whether a female analyst would come back from *maternity* leave to an embrace of *paternity* leave. But we'll continue to remind the men we work with that just because your wife chose to stay home after she had kids doesn't mean we will.

Conclusion: Psychocultural Barriers Will Only Fall with Greater Diversity

We hope that this chapter showed you how a set of interrelated, psychocultural factors inherent to the current structure of IM conspires to block women's progress in it. Traits more associated with men— confidence, risk-taking, and ambition—are perceived to be critical to good investment results, despite a lack of evidence for this. These misconceptions lead to "low-value seats" and promotion delays which means that our track records are likely shorter than those of our male peers. Male-skewed networking events and office politics disadvantage our salient minority. And a "SAHW" culture in which stay-at-home-wives are the norm lead some senior colleagues and, more important, those who are supposed to sponsor and advocate for us to look at us differently.

It's no wonder women are a fraction of our numbers.

Happily, we heard lots of women express optimism that things are changing, with anecdotes ranging from a paternity leave push to better support systems for women in the industry. We are optimistic as well, but cognizant of the raw numbers that show that since the 2008 financial crisis, there are *fewer* female PMs. And if market downturns are disproportionately hard on women in IM, the COVID-19 pandemic may take yet another whack at our numbers.

There is hope! We're about to embark upon a deep dive into the work-life balance issues faced by women in our industry—and here, we think we stack up well against some of our professional female colleagues outside investing. After that, we will introduce you to some role models who provide evidence that these barriers are surmountable— and might even be starting to crumble. The grim good news is that active investment management is long overdue for a cultural rethink in light of its share loss and declining profitability. Tearing down IM's insidious, psychocultural obstacles to women is a great place to start.

7

Your Portfolio Is Balanced—Your Life Can Be, Too!

Debunking the Work–Life Balance Myth in IM

Careful readers will note that we did not include the work–life balance subject in the prior chapter about barriers to women's success in IM. That is because we do not view it as any more of a barrier for the majority of investing jobs than it is in corporate America. We recognize that the intensity of some asset classes and IM firm cultures—such as with certain types of hedge fund and smaller, lean investment managers—can create an environment where work–life balance is aspirational rather than achievable. However, as one of us with a very good work–life balance at a small firm can attest, even some small firms are good places to find balance.

Our work–life balance hypothesis was corroborated by our primary research. By and large, the women we spoke with echoed a comment we shared with you earlier: "I know oodles of women in investment banking and more face-time-oriented roles in finance who quit because they couldn't figure out work–life balance. But in investment management, I've literally never known a woman portfolio manager who quit because she couldn't figure this out."

We hope to encourage any of you who are worried that you can't "figure this out" by providing lots of examples proving that balance is not only desirable but achievable in IM. Although we are by no means saying that women in IM have an average of 2.6 perfect kids and sail through life doing triathlons with a home that rivals Martha Stewart's, we want to leave you with the confidence to pursue the career even if you are also committed to having, and spending time with, a family and/or having an exciting social life. And we want to be sure you get the message that once you reach a "cruising altitude" of good results and credibility at your firm, this career can offer better balance than some others. Here are a few other quotes that echo this perspective.

> This job is outcome oriented. It's not like how many hours were you in the office? It's about, what did you produce for your clients?

> I hear "you can't have a balanced lifestyle if you're a PM" a lot—I think that's BS. It's driven by market hours—you don't have to stay until midnight finishing a pitchbook.

> I think that whether you're a concert pianist or an architect, to do really well, you have to work a lot of hours. And so that comes into play in any profession, and I think asset management is actually easier because I don't need to have a baby grand to work. I just need to have my Excel models and computer.

> We have more flexible working [hours] than in pretty much any other industry.

It's not just our interviewees who believe that work–life balance is achievable in money management. A 2016 CFA Institute study found that a majority of men and women (66 percent and 63 percent, respectively) said that it wasn't hard to take time off when working in IM. This is slightly but not significantly lower than the general U.S. population (76 percent of men and 70 percent of women with college degrees agree). Both genders also found that it was relatively easy to adjust their hours (that is, what time they start and finish), which is the easiest way to balance career demands with other interests, be it children, competing in a marathon, or elderly parents.

Let's Start with the Bad News—It's Tough to Be a Working Mother

We recognize the challenges that working mothers in senior roles face. We face them ourselves. These challenges arise at home and at work. Research has shown that despite all the claims of how cool it is to be a new-age guy who contributes at home and splits childcare duties 50–50 with his partner, women still take on most of the childcare and other domestic responsibilities. Even the "good" guys leave childcare to their wives; according to one study,[1] men who pulled their weight before kids arrived significantly pulled back after the kids came along—by as much as a five-hour/week reduction in their contributions to the household. Post-kids, more of the burden shifted to women. It seems like every five minutes there's a new study showing this. For example, a February 2020 *New York Times* article entitled "How to Make Your Marriage Gayer" cited a plethora of studies that can be summarized as follows: heterosexual married women make up the demographic that experiences the most stress at home—and this stress is directly correlated with how little their husbands do around that home, whether housework or childcare.[2] More recently, in a reversal of decades of progress, it appears that the COVID-19 pandemic's work-from-home transition is shifting family burdens disproportionately back onto the shoulders of women (sample headline: "When Mom's Zoom Meeting Is the One That Has to Wait," *New York Times*, April 22, 2020).

As another *New York Times* article notes, "Whether women work at Walmart or on Wall Street, getting pregnant is often the moment [women] are knocked off the professional ladder. In fact, it

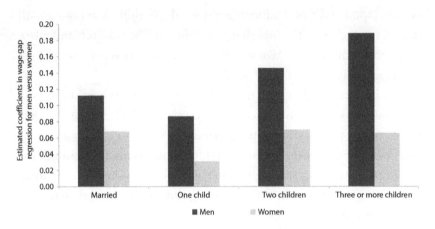

FIGURE 7.1 Marriage and children affect women's and men's earnings differently. This graph shows the impact of marriage and parenthood on the wage rate for prime working-age men versus women.

Source: IPUMS-CPS, Goldman Sachs Global Investment Research.

is between mothers and non-mothers that the pay gap is most significant."[3] Why? We agree with Eve Rodsky, the author of *Fair Play*, that this is partly because women become the "she-fault" parent, the one who takes on more responsibilities after children arrive, the one the school nurse calls when the kids are sick. (And yes, both of your authors have been there—they can find our cell numbers, but for some reason they can't find those of our baby-daddies—and yes, both numbers are on file.)

Goldman Sachs data shows that marriage and children affect men and women in different ways. According to Goldman's analysis, a married male with children is paid more because he has "greater responsibilities" (aka his SAHW) than a married female with children (fig. 7.1).[4]

This analysis shows only correlation, not causality. However, it echoes a story one of us heard about how to craft a compelling résumé to land a public company board position. A man who includes "married with four children" is congratulated, whereas a woman is perceived as having too much on her plate to be able to take on additional board responsibilities. Unfortunately, we don't think leaving kids off résumés will change the fact that, according to the research and advocacy organization 2020 Women on Boards, only 22.6 percent of Russell 3000 board members are women.[5]

We cite these studies (and nod to the many, many others) to remind you that working women face a unique set of challenges when they take on responsibility for another person, whether a child, aging parent, or sick spouse. Our intent with this chapter is not to minimize the difficulty of walking this tightrope but, rather, to show that women in IM have as good a shot of managing these competing demands as women in other industries.

How Do Working PM Moms Do It?
There Are Prototypes, Plural

As you have read, your coauthors have very different living situations. One of us lives in New York with four kids (which she had as she was building her career) and a working husband. The other was married to her job until she had an "oops" baby at age forty and now telecommutes from Asheville, North Carolina, with joint custody of her only child (a situation she refers to as having half a child). These paths are two of several prototypes of successful work–life balancers we will describe here—and, as in our constellation chapter, they are meant to give you an array of ways to be successful, not *the* way.

Prototype 1: The Parallel-Pathers

This is the prototype that makes you say with reverence (as in the movie of the same title), "I don't know how she does it." Ellen frequently makes this observation of Katrina, who falls into this category. These are the women who call in trades from the delivery room. They have children early in their careers, with partners who also have demanding jobs (this makes them "assortative maters"). They grow their careers and families in parallel. It's by no means easy to do this, as the deck can be stacked against women who get pregnant "too early" (by some indeterminate standard—we hope you remember our composite character Tanya from chapter 6). And some see their marriages end in divorce, which can either reduce the home demands (with actual, 50–50 joint custody) or increase them, with custody that is joint in name only—let's call this "JINO," with apologies for the sound of it—that shifts the majority of the burden to the mother. We'll let them tell you some of their stories.

I would pray that I wouldn't get sick before an international research trip.

My kids owned me on weekends and evenings.

My parents ended up moving to Geneva with me to help with my three- and five-year-old sons. I slept on the living room couch.

Prototype 2: The Sequencers

This is Ellen's prototype. These women establish themselves and transition from analyst to PM before having kids. The benefit of this is obvious: it's much easier to carve out time for your family once you've built a track record of performance and credibility with your investment team. It's hard to be pregnant or the mother of a baby while you're trying to prove yourself as a PM; how do you compare results after a three-month maternity leave gap with the uninterrupted work of other PMs? The downside risk is obvious as well: if a woman waits too long to have kids, she runs out of time biologically. Think of this approach as landing an airplane on an aircraft carrier rather than a runway; you have to be very precise with your timing, and you can't control the weather. But when it works, this sequential approach can fit well into the PM promotional cadence, as evidenced by the voices below. Unfortunately, with the declining number of actively managed funds and resultant increasing competition for PM roles, we think the analyst-to-PM path could take longer in the future, which further works against women's biological clocks.

A mentor told me, you can have it all, just not at the same time . . . waiting a little bit [to have kids] was great because now I have quite a bit more time and can really enjoy my son and have more time with him now.

I was fortunate to have landed in the career [so that] when I decided I was going to have children I was already in my career.

I did my life backward. I had my child and my marriage late in my career.

Prototype 3: The SAHD Moms

Women who have children with spouses who embrace staying home with the kids are well represented in our industry. As mentioned earlier, this is a privilege of working in a career that is well paid.

My husband has given up his job, which is great.

For the last seven years, my husband has been a full-time dad. I don't think you have to have that to be successful in investment management, but I cannot discount the extent to which that is a privilege that I've had that was certainly helpful.

Prototype 4: The Married-to-Jobbers

Finally, there are women in our industry who don't have spouses or kids. (As one of our interviewees put it, "I don't have kids, I have cats.") A recent book corroborates earlier studies that have found this demographic to be the happiest.[6] And the gender pay gap shrinks meaningfully for single men and women.[7]

One interesting theme among this cohort is a sense of chicken and egg; did they choose to be single because they liked their careers so much and didn't want to make time for a family, or were they avowedly single or childless early on and pursued this career because it fulfilled them? As one of our interviewees put it, "I'm single with no kids. I don't know if it's a consequence of my career or my life." One of us, who almost stayed married to the job (and was rescued, or waylaid, by an "oops" baby), can appreciate this sentiment. The job can be so, well, fun that it kindles a type of passion that crowds out other passions. One of our industry opt-outs, who happily and voluntarily retired from her PM job after having kids, said that talking to people who still work at her old company is like seeing an old boyfriend walking down the street. It always elicits a pang of nostalgia and a sense of "the one who got away."

Another interesting theme in this cohort is a sense of modesty or even self-deprecation. As one of our interviewees put it, "I don't have children. So I can't appreciate entirely some of the difficulties which my colleagues who do have children go through. I can only imagine it is incredibly difficult." Single women can suffer from a type of impostor syndrome—the sense that they are underachievers relative to their peers with spouses and/or kids, and that if they had had to "do it all," they wouldn't have done as well. Yet we know that although single women aren't balancing kids, they might have to balance elderly parents, nieces and nephews, and other relationships that are no less important.

We hope that the message you've gotten throughout this chapter is that it might, in fact, be less incredibly difficult than it appears from the outside to balance your work and life as a PM. The challenges to women in IM are more likely to arise at work than at home.

We Can't Leave This Discussion Without a Shout-Out to All the Supportive Family Members Who Help Us

We want to make sure that all the family members (primarily, but not exclusively, husbands) who support our interviewees get their due, so here are some great quotes.

> Work–life balance has not been an issue for me because I have a very supportive husband.

> It's important to marry well. . . . My husband is incredibly supportive and good-natured. . . . Part of [my success] is my husband . . . his support and helping me pursue this while we also have two great kids.

> You need a tremendous amount of support at home. I had it and it was difficult, but I think the line between difficult and impossible becomes all about that type of support from home—your husband, your family situation, whatever it is.

On behalf of our interviewees, thank you, "Lean In" spouses. Whether you work outside the home or stay there with the kids, we women recognize your contributions (in, perhaps, a way that men don't celebrate stay-at-home wives). Those of us who don't enjoy the same support salute our peers who show both men and women that traditional gender roles are dissolving. And thank you to all the grandparents, extended family, paid caregivers, and other people who help our kids and pets thrive (or, at least, keep them alive) while we're staying late at the office, traveling for a research trip, or having dinner with a client.

Flexibility: The Silver Bullet?

We'll end this chapter in a way that might seem contradictory to its primary message: with a plea for greater flexibility for *all* people in IM. Despite the quotes about flexibility at the beginning of this chapter, we don't want to leave you with the impression that flexible and remote-working situations are the norm. Although the pandemic has required many firms, IM included, to permit (and even mandate) virtual working, it's unclear whether this flexibility becomes the norm post-COVID-19. One of us telecommutes, but this is not typical; as you might remember from chapter 2, the investment management model is built around teams of analysts, traders, and PMs in one place, exchanging information during market hours that might lead to investment decisions. Leaving aside the question of whether the concept of market hours is relevant to investing, given that work needs to be done both during and outside trading hours, it is worth asking: Why can't the PM role be part-time, or job-shared, or otherwise flexible? The irony of this question is that at the best firms, which value investment performance and cultural contributions over face time, the PM role can in fact be rather . . . part-time. This is echoed by the quotes at the beginning of the chapter.

How many hours does it take to beat the index? This answer is different for every PM; there is no standard response. We have met successful PMs who are at their desks ten or more hours per day and catch up on reading broker reports on the weekends. We have met an equal number of PMs who are at their desks half of that time and who manage to get their reading done during office hours to boot— yet would not dare to mention this to a boss or client, or on the record for this book. A better mousetrap—that is, an analytical process and investment approach that lead to superior results—can decrease the number of hours required to do the job well. In fact, a few of the women we interviewed chose the PM over the analyst track for its flexibility. (The analyst role is a servicing one, versus the PM, who expects to be serviced.) Yet the image and idolatry of the workaholic PM persists, both in the industry and outside it.

We know from various studies that women place a higher value on flexibility than men. A 2018 study by the staff of the Federal Reserve Bank of New York analyzed the preferences for job attributes by gender and found that women are lost during child-bearing years from jobs that do not support flexible work and family leave.[8] This is borne out within the CFA ranks: "Female CFA members are 75 percent more likely than a male CFA to choose a reduction in pay and hours. . . . [M]arriage and children affect women's desire to recapture time from work, but not men's."[9] Allowing people—men *and* women—to work remotely, flexibly, and/or in part-time job-sharing structures could expand the PM career opportunity to a broader demographic without impairing results. This requires setting the tone at the top; department heads, research managers, and the like need to support and utilize this flexibility to turn it into a culture.

As one of our interviewees told us, "Historically remote work wasn't fully accepted or embraced, but these days technology makes it very easy to be remote. The cultural shift is still a work in progress." We will leave you with this thought: if IM firms can become bleeding edge on remote and flexible working arrangements for women *and* men who place a high value on it, imagine how much bigger the talent pool could become.

8

The Constellation

Discussions with Successful Women in Investment Management

By now you've heard so much about barriers to women in IM that you might be wondering how any of us is still standing. This chapter is about the ones who made it. As PMs who have worked at several IM firms in our collective forty years in the industry, we represent the salient minority. Our decades of experience as investors opened doors for us to interview some of the top female PMs. Although we will never know the precise reason that each of them decided to speak to us, most of them in on-the-record interviews, we can highlight a few points that we think tipped the balance in our favor and will give many aspiring investors, particularly women, the inspiration to pursue a career in our engaging, stimulating, and lucrative field.

The first is that every woman we interviewed was referred to us through someone we know. In addition to current and past colleagues, we had referrals from mutual fund board trustees, former nonprofit board members, and other tangential industry connections. This willingness to make crucial introductions and vouch for us as first-time authors was invaluable. Second, as PMs ourselves, we understand how to work with corporate PR teams and the value of one's personal reputation and the reputation of one's firm. Where necessary we have anonymized quotes, not because we are protecting the guilty but to ensure that both sides of the story are told—the stories of the successful and of those opting out. Finally, when speaking with potential interviewees, we were clear that this book is not about blaming men. Many of our interviewees are in their seats because they were supported, mentored, or sponsored by successful male investors. Our optimistic approach of finding solutions rather than trying to blame the industry for past mistakes was in line with our interviewees' own thinking in most cases.

Our analysis of these interviews, in which we utilized a set of fifteen standardized questions, has three angles. We employed a statistical, quantitative approach to analyze the answers using natural-language processing to determine commonality among our interviewees. We have also used positive/negative testing. Finally, we have mined our interview transcripts to surface some interesting quotes and perspectives that we believe will help aspiring and current PMs learn from successful industry participants.

The Lack of a Female North Star

Our profession needs a female North Star, and we don't have one yet.

—RUPAL BHANSALI, CHIEF INVESTMENT OFFICER, INTERNATIONAL
AND GLOBAL EQUITIES, ARIEL INVESTMENTS

We do lack a kind of Northern Star in terms of a female PM like a female Warren Buffett—there isn't one.

—LAURA GERITZ, FOUNDER, CEO AND PORTFOLIO MANAGER,
RONDURE GLOBAL ADVISORS

Research has proven that female role models increase women's willingness to compete.[1] Investing is, by definition, a competitive job—remember, success is all about beating a benchmark—so the impact of female role models in our industry is particularly high. Numerous studies have found that female role models mitigate gender stereotype threats and lead to higher self-confidence among women. In light of the confidence gap we discussed in chapter 6,[2] the presence of such role models in IM could potentially have a double benefit to women in the industry: it not only helps women believe in themselves, it also provides them with a realistic benchmark (all important in IM!) against which to measure their progress.

To state the obvious, having few women at the top of any organization creates a cycle that is difficult to disrupt. It starts at recruitment and goes all the way to the boardroom.

    a. Few female senior leaders in an organization means fewer aspirational role models, which makes it difficult to recruit entry-level analysts.

    b. Fewer female entry-level analysts results in a salient minority that depresses female retention rates because the culture feels less friendly.

    c. Lower female retention rates mean there are fewer women to promote to middle management (senior analysts and portfolio managers).

    d. Fewer women in middle management begets fewer female senior leaders.

And the cycle goes on.

We want to break this cycle, and we believe that providing an industry touchstone for aspiring women is critical.

Who is our North Star? We admit to considering whether we should self-anoint as the industry's joint North Stars (we are coauthors who believe in sharing everything equally). Ultimately, we decided against designating any female in the industry as a lone North Star. As we mentioned earlier, Warren Buffett became the world's most famous investor well before the 24/7 news cycle, the selfie, and the Twitter-sphere. The PM role is already a high-pressure position; singling out one woman, no matter how amazing her results and career, to be our industry standard-bearer seems unfair and unnecessary. For perspective on this, just imagine the press coverage: "Don't navigate by this female 'North Star'—her portfolio was down 10 percent last year." As we hope you know by now, occasionally being spectacularly wrong is an occupational hazard of the PM role; if you run a big fund, your numbers are public—and the trolling is easy.

More important, there are—happily!—so many candidates for this North Star position (ourselves excluded) that we couldn't choose among them. They all have different backgrounds, different paths to success, different reasons they continued in this field, and different strengths, and, yes, weaknesses. And we want *any* woman considering an IM career, be it an undergraduate, MBA student, or even a career switcher, to see the diversity of women who have been successful and are at the top of their game. They represent a mix of backgrounds and personal choices—some single, some in same-sex relationships, and some married. Some of them have children, some don't, and some haven't decided yet. One started as a receptionist, another as a reporter. Many came into IM through the more typical MBA channels. They are all different, yet each has been immensely successful, and hence we celebrate them not as individuals but as a constellation made up of many bright stars.

Our Constellation Shines Bright

A constellation is a set of stars that unite into a recognizable form. The women we interviewed—the stars in our constellation—shared their stories and strategies for success in IM. Our analysis of the interview transcripts identified a pattern of commonalities that helped our interviewees become successful PMs. Their advice is relevant to an undergraduate considering this career, an MBA enrolled in her first class on securities analysis, and an analyst wanting to transition to a PM role.

We deliberately do *not* say "successful in a man's world" because we believe that the attributes of our interviewees' success will help any aspiring PM become successful. We believe that their timeless advice, which we share below verbatim, will be equally relevant even when the PM role reaches gender parity. And because we have many female friends outside IM, we believe that some of the advice might apply to those of you in other industries.

The Important Role of Mentors and Sponsors

Over 85 percent of the women we interviewed had mentors. "My mentors have always been men," said Barbara Ann Bernard, founder of her own IM firm and the Variant Perspectives conference, which was headlined by Warren Buffet in its inaugural year. Although male mentors were the norm for some of our interviewees, many of the women had both male and female mentors. Not everyone we interviewed was fortunate enough to have mentors; many wished that they did. Some found other ways to get the advice and inspiration they needed to move forward in their career.

Elena Khoziaeva's advice to aspiring PMs was to "find mentors . . . it's important." Lauren Taylor Wolfe, who recently cofounded the activist hedge fund Impactive Capital, told us, "One thing I regret is not seeking out more mentors." Jane Buchan, who founded her own hedge fund, Martlet Asset Management, said, "I've had outstanding mentorship" when talking about the reasons for her very successful career. Kelly Thomas, an equity analyst at Jennison, attributes her success as an analyst to her mentors, as does Kristi Mitchem, the head of BMO's asset management division: "I had absolutely fantastic mentorship and sponsorship really throughout my career."

Despite the lack of women in IM, Saira Malik, chief investment officer and head of Nuveen Equities, highlights the importance of her female mentors to her highly successful career in this business:

[The female head of research] said to me, "You can one day be like me, head of research." I remember just looking at her thinking, what are you talking about? And then I remember thinking, wait a minute, she's a woman, older than me, but she started as a steel analyst. I was a chemicals analyst. We actually don't look that different, right?

However, not everyone has been as fortunate as Ms. Malik. One successful PM told us,

I've never had a female mentor and honestly, women have been more of an obstacle in my career than a help. I'm hoping that this is changing. But when I was young and trying to develop these relationships, I think that a lot of women felt that there was only one seat at the table, and they wanted it for themselves.

We need to distinguish between having a North Star and having mentors and sponsors for women. A woman who fits the criteria of a North Star can be a mentor and sponsor to junior women in the organization, but there are not enough senior women in the industry for only women to sponsor and mentor women. Men need to step up to the plate as well. If we want to address the gender diversity gap, both men and women need to mentor and sponsor more women in the earlier parts of their careers. Given that sponsors and mentors (and recall the different role that each plays in your career) were instrumental in the careers of many successful women, these efforts need to accelerate in our industry.

The Child Prodigies

I have known I wanted to be a stock picker since I was 18.
—ANNA DOPKIN, STRATEGIC PROJECT MANAGER AT T. ROWE PRICE AND FORMER PORTFOLIO MANAGER

I have wanted to manage money for as long as I can remember. My favorite movie was *Pretty Woman* . . . because I wanted to be Richard Gere!
—BARBARA ANN BERNARD, FOUNDER OF WINCREST CAPITAL

My father was a stockbroker, so I grew up hearing stock stories when my peers were probably into fairy tales.

—RUPAL BHANSALI, CHIEF INVESTMENT OFFICER, INTERNATIONAL AND GLOBAL EQUITIES, ARIEL INVESTMENTS

In chapter 5 we referenced the stereotypical (male) MBA who knew he wanted to buy and sell stocks practically in utero. We found some female examples of this as well in our interviews, women whose mothers signed off on their brokerage trades and who used the Warren Buffett "buy what you know approach" to identify the stock that benefits from the middle-school fashion trends she observes. However, these examples were the exception rather than the rule.

Not all of us emerged from the womb reading *The Wall Street Journal*. Both of your authors grew up in "land-rich, cash-poor" families; all of our families' assets were invested in real estate and real estate–related businesses. There was not a stock to be seen. We heard similar feedback from many of our interviewees. As Clare Hart at JP Morgan Asset Management told us, "A lot of new college grads talk about how they've been reading *The Wall Street Journal* since they were twelve. They have their own portfolios. I didn't know anything about Wall Street before I got there." And Sarah Ketterer, founder of Causeway Capital—and daughter of another successful PM—told us, "I literally went into the business in spite of my father."

Although we salute the kids who take the initiative to buy SBUX before they're old enough to drink coffee because they have watched their parents search desperately for their caffeine fix, we feel that the recruiting process over-rewards a candidate with these types of investment stories at the expense of more diverse backgrounds, for two reasons. First, the demographic of kids who are exposed to the markets, and have disposable wealth to invest in them, is narrow. Second, studies show that parents generally spend more time talking with boys about finance than with girls—even in the same family, daughters don't get the same exposure to investing as their brothers. We'll talk about this more in our solutions section.

Persistence and Perseverance—Obvious, But Cannot Be Overstated in IM

Your authors have stayed with this career for decades, as have many of the other PMs we interviewed. We cannot overstate the importance of understanding that there are many bad days in IM; that's just part of the job. A good analyst will never bat 100 percent with her stock picks—she will always get something wrong. And a good PM is going to have years when she doesn't beat her benchmark. You can be right on your investment thesis but wrong on something completely unknowable and unrelated (hello, COVID-19). "The market can stay irrational longer than you can stay solvent," said John Maynard Keynes, and we couldn't agree more. Neither of us packed up and went home when we had a bad day, year, or market cycle.

Our interviewees agree with the need for a PM to have resilience in the face of down markets. In their words, "persistence, perseverance, and sticking with it," according to Ulrike Hoffmann-Burchardi, PM at Tudor Investment Corporation, are vital for succeeding as a PM. Clare Hart at JP Morgan Asset Management echoed some quotes from chapter 6 when she told us,

> I used to think, if you need the justification or that pat on the back to feel like you're doing a good job, this is not the career for you because the market will just kick you around. Now I realize that is true of any demanding industry. The reality is, especially as a woman on Wall Street, you have to take your own counsel and make your own decisions. Don't wait for anyone to pat you on the back.

Maria Negrete said, "Every day the market will tell you how you are doing." Even longer-term investors, who have the luxury of time, still need to get their stock calls right in the long run. And when something goes against you, you need to know when to throw in the towel.

Sandy Miller told us, "You have to be willing to accept when you were wrong, learn from your mistake, and move on." Michelle Clayman highlighted how "some have the stomach for it and some don't."

Many PMs also attributed their success to hard work. Ann-Marie Griffith, managing director at APG Asset Management US, Inc., perhaps stated the obvious when she told us that "this is a demanding career." The intensity compounds the need for perseverance; as Anastasia Titarchuk, CIO of the New York Common Retirement Fund, put it, "It's an intense industry. Just realize that it's going to be a lot of work and a lot of people telling you that you don't know something."

Yet as you know from the prior chapter, although IM can involve long hours, it is generally not a more demanding job than other high-powered careers that have achieved greater gender parity. We heard repeatedly in our interviewees with successful PMs that although work–life balance was something they had to consider, they did not view it as a barrier to the successful pursuit of an IM career.

The Role of Luck

Luck is typically personified as female ("Luck, be a lady tonight"), so perhaps it's no surprise that many of our interviewees mentioned luck as a contributor to their success. We don't want to overemphasize its role in creating successful PMs (hard work is necessary too), but we mention luck here for two reasons. First, we believe it is disingenuous for any investor with good results to say that luck played no role in her career. Daniel Kahneman's book *Thinking Fast and Slow* is a great distillation of many studies showing that successful people vastly underestimate the role that luck has played in their careers.[3] We would argue that this is even more true in investing, as markets move in mysterious and random ways. Second, although we don't have a comparable sample size, we suspect that fewer men than women would mention the role of luck in their investment success.

Recommending This Career: Should You Pursue It?

I think it's a fabulous career for women and I think that women are extremely well suited to it.

—MELISSA O'CONNOR CASSON, DIRECTOR OF GLOBAL EQUITIES, BLACK CREEK INVESTMENT MANAGEMENT

Four of five of the women whom we interviewed would recommend this career to their daughters (or hypothetical daughters, for those without them). Anna Dopkin, strategic project manager at T. Rowe Price and former portfolio manager, summed it up best when she said she would recommend it to her daughter "in a heartbeat." Her message was consistent across our cohort of interviewees. Some qualified their answer by saying they would direct a daughter into this career only if she were interested in finance.

For the minority who wouldn't recommend that their daughters pursue IM, many focused on the significant changes the industry is undergoing and highlighted the uncertainties facing the IM industry that we discussed in the first chapter: the rise of passive investing and the increasing use of technology. This was a gender-neutral perspective— equally applicable to sons and daughters. Although we share these concerns, we believe that increasing diversity might be an effective way to address these uncertainties.

"I Made It"

We asked women at all points in their portfolio management careers if they felt like they had made it. Some were recently appointed to their roles, and others were industry veterans. The number of women who answered this in the affirmative could be counted on one hand. Many of us have celebrated "short-term victory laps" (according to

Jane Buchan of Martlet Asset Management), but for the most part we are still looking for that next challenge.

Taking Risks in Their Careers

"We as women sometimes don't take enough risks with our careers. We need to take those risks, and I forced myself often to take steps that were sometimes pretty uncomfortable." Sonal Desai is the head of fixed income at Franklin Templeton Investments, and she makes a point that we heard many times throughout our research: women don't take as many risks in their careers as men do. Risk-taking is hard to teach, but taking risks is often the reason that many people in very successful positions got there. "This is definitely a career where fortune favors the brave," said Anne Christine Farstad, a portfolio manager at MFS. Barbara Miller, a successful PM at Federated Hermes, told us, "I think I'd be twice as successful if I took more risk."

For women looking to move ahead, Margo Cook, CFA, former president at Nuveen Advisory Services, advises,

> Taking risks in your career is so critical and something that many women are reluctant to do. Make sure your voice is heard on the company's strategy, ask for new responsibilities in your current role, and seek a new role within your organization; taking calculated risks helps to move ahead. If women get more comfortable taking risks, they'll see the rewards that follow.

You don't have to act like a guy to succeed. Even if you do, you will probably be asked to get coffee.

> I've had a lot of advice to behave more like the guys. (Laura Geritz, founder, CEO, and portfolio manager, Rondure Global Advisors)

I have a PhD from Harvard. I have led one of the biggest funds-of-funds. I am still shocked by the amount of time that I am proverbially asked to get coffee. (Jane Buchan, CEO and co-CIO, Martlet Asset Management)

These quotes bookend the conflicting expectations of women in IM. On one hand, we are told to "act more like guys" to network more effectively. On the other hand, when it's time to organize something, whether it's the office holiday party or a new intern program, women get asked to do the job.

You don't have to act like a guy to be successful in IM, but you do have to be able to hold your own—and it doesn't hurt if you can do what the guys enjoy doing. "Bill Miller taught me how to smoke a cigar," recalled the late Cindy Sweeting, former CIO at Franklin Templeton Investments. We can personally attest to the value of cigar smoking, poker playing, and other typically male pursuits in IM.

We are not advising that you adopt this behavior. When you are in a room with nine men and you're the lonely female, it is easy to just want to be one of the guys. We wrote this book to make this advice anachronistic. Once we cross that salient minority barrier, there will be at least three of us in each room of ten investors. While the guys hit the golf course, some of us might head to Soul-Cycle and even convince the golf-hating men in the room to join us. (Happily, one of your authors has seen this happen already—and her male cohort didn't seem to mind being the salient minority in the class.)

Career Coaches and HR Departments

I am the product, for better or worse, of a lot of coaching and career development activity.

—MELANIE DAVIS, CHIEF INVESTMENT OFFICER OF A FAMILY OFFICE AND FORMERLY A SENIOR EXECUTIVE AT AIG

Only 36 percent of our interviewees received career coaching or participated in a career training program that helped them move forward. One of us began as a consultant at one of the large accounting firms, where career development and manager training programs are well established and form an integral part of an employee's career development at these firms. Today, according to Catalyst, more than half (61 percent) of all accountants and auditors are women. This is a staggering increase from 39 percent in 1983. Although only 24 percent of partners are female, that is a higher percentage than our 10 percent of PMs. And with a strong and growing pipeline of women in the industry, as well as programs that support the career development of these employees, we would expect to see increasing diversity at the top levels of accounting firms.[4]

Whitney Tilson, a retired hedge fund manager, gave us an interesting perspective. He seconded the advice to women that he heard from a female industry friend: "Only work at a firm with an HR department—this is a good litmus test for whether women might get a fair shake." We noted earlier in the book that hedge funds have even worse gender metrics than the industry overall, and one contributor to this imbalance is that aside from the large, well-known ones, hedge funds tend to be small and thus lack HR departments. We would agree with the spirit of our interviewee's advice, if not the letter; one of us works for a small investment manager without an HR department, but because it happens to be majority woman-owned with a female CEO, it's female-friendly. Our advice: do your research on the firms with which you interview.

Advice from Successful Portfolio Managers and Analysts

In the next chapter, where we tell our own stories, we have included some advice for women in the industry or considering it. As a prelude, we thought that we would conclude this chapter with some great advice that our successful PMs and analysts were willing to share with you.

Act like you're supposed to be there. (Kelly Thomas, managing director and equity analyst, Jennison Associates LLC)

Don't take no for an answer . . . you have to be a little scrappy and shameless to make things work. (Lauren Taylor Wolfe, cofounder and managing partner, Impactive Capital)

Speak up, keep speaking in meetings. (Sonal Desai, CIO, Fixed Income Group, Franklin Templeton)

Use your voice. . . . I always say if you want something, ask for it. For example, ask for more responsibility if you want to be challenged, and raise your hand, because you know that your male counterpart is asking for more. (Janet King, managing director, First Manhattan Co.)

Find the right balance between humility and conviction. (Melissa O'Connor Casson, director of global equities, Black Creek Investment Management)

What About the Opt-Outs?

When we set out to write this book, we envisioned a whole chapter on "opt-outs"—women who decided to leave the IM industry—thinking that their experiences and counsel would provide valuable solutions to the industry's gender imbalance. However, that chapter dissolved into a few paragraphs as we ran up against several barriers to this approach.

First, there simply aren't that many female analysts and PMs who have left the industry. As you have heard repeatedly, it's hard to get these IM jobs, and the women who end up in them generally know what they're in for. Once they succeed, they are unlikely to leave.

We do, however, know women personally (and were referred to others in our interviews) who self-selected out of IM, and here we ran up against another barrier: many declined our interview request due to confidentiality agreements, or a fear of burning bridges or of being labeled a failure. And some who opted out of IM have continued to use their skills in their new professions. As one opt-out told us, "I wasn't impressed by the [IM] company I joined, and I ended up leaving the IM industry and moved into an internal M&A department at a public company." (And would she recommend the career to her daughter? "Yes, absolutely.") Another opt-out told us, "I found myself in an industry in cyclical and secular decline"—a view that we understand but believe has room for interpretation. As discussed in the prologue, although passive strategies have taken hold, there are many growing areas of active management. And we will footnote the earlier quote by mentioning that our interviewee is now a successful analyst at a private wealth manager, using financial technology to help the clients she now serves.

One of our opt-out contacts could not be interviewed given her new career, but she told us how valuable the skills she gained as an analyst are—including financial modeling, strategic analysis, and the process of piecing together mosaics of information to form a conclusion. These skills can be utilized in many roles—M&A, investment banking, strategy, and management consulting, to name a few. All these roles are knowledge based, with ever-changing projects and the ability to continuously learn—characteristics that identify both successful PMs and more broadly successful knowledge-based workers. We cite her experience to encourage those of you who are thinking about the career but are worried about some of the structural barriers to women we've discussed. You might end up with a toolbox of skills that positions you for your next career.

Finally, we have to acknowledge—and celebrate—one small group of opt-outs: women who made enough money as high-performing PMs to retire in their fifties and even forties. Although we want to be careful not to misrepresent anecdotes as data, we struggle to think of any male PMs who have left because they had "enough" money—but can name several women who have. As one opt-out told us, "When I said I was leaving, my male co-workers asked, 'How can you afford to do that?' My answer was: 'How can you *not* afford to leave?' "

Our Call to Action

Sarah Ketterer, cofounder, CEO, and PM at Causeway Capital Management, believes that "women are intimidated because there are so few role models." We hope, after reading this chapter, that you will now disagree with her statement. There are plenty of role models— you just haven't heard of them until now. We have interviewed more than fifty successful women investors, and we know many more in the industry. Our message to aspiring PMs is to look up at the constellation of successful women in IM.

To those female PMs who have made it, whether you admit to this or not—as a newly anointed member of the North Star constellation, not only should you continue to shine, but you should also recognize that you are the inspiration for many. We challenge you to step up to the plate as the role models who women need and who we know you can be. Participate in visibility campaigns and support the initiatives that we detail in later chapters. Highlighting your success is integral to breaking the cycle we outlined at the beginning of this chapter.

9

How Did We Succeed in Investment Management?

Our Different Paths to Successful IM Careers

We have briefly talked about our different career paths from analyst to PM. Different personal situations have influenced your authors' individual career journeys as a parallel-pather (Katrina) and a sequencer (Ellen). Both of us entered the industry with MBAs from well-known schools, one with an accounting background, the other a literature background. One was on the partner track at an accounting firm before pursuing an IM career; the other one was giving it a year to decide whether she enjoyed it.

After more than twenty years each in the industry, we can both say that we have enjoyed our time as analysts and, later, PMs. Along the way we have met, worked with, and sought career advice from many capable women in IM—colleagues and friends who have been there to inspire and guide us. By sharing our stories, we don't want to be seen to substitute for the constellation of women who we profiled in the preceding chapter; rather, we want to provide a more detailed look at how two women succeeded in a male-dominated industry.

As career women, we have been surprised at the willingness of both men and women to give us advice on how to succeed—and the lack of similar proclamations for our male friends and colleagues, as though they were born with a built-in career navigation gene and had no need of advice. We have been told that we can "have it all" and that we "can't have it all," and told to "lean in" and "lean out." So instead of providing aspiring PMs with more, perhaps unnecessary and almost certainly repetitive, advice, we thought that we'd share some things we wish we'd known when we started. These are our stories, not roadmaps; as you learned in the prior chapter, there are many paths to becoming a PM. Here are ours.

Katrina's Career Journey

I always liked numbers. Math and any subject that involved calculations were my favorites in school. Although it was unusual for a girl, I thought that accounting was fun, and business intrigued me. Like many kids with mathematical aptitude, I also loved to play music— from the piano to the saxophone and violin. But in the ninth grade I was forced to choose between a concentration in music and business. I chose the latter, my first step toward a career in IM. One of the key skills that I learned at this early age was balancing risk and reward: although business can be risky, there are multiple opportunities to succeed, so it's a fairly balanced risk-reward trade-off. In music, success is a one-in-a-million chance. The ability to weigh risk and reward has served me well throughout my investment career.

I grew up in Australia, and my father was an entrepreneur. He didn't own stocks and bonds; he owned a company that built houses—lots of them. I didn't realize that you could have a part interest in a company until I got to college and studied finance. I thought that either you owned it all or you had a partner and shared everything—50-50, of course. Unlike the students who interview today with stories about childhood investments, I was not a child prodigy.

As you read earlier, my path to IM was not via your typical U.S. four-year college education followed by a two-year investment banking job and then a two-year full-time MBA program. In college in Australia, I studied commerce and law and got degrees in both (in

Australia, a law degree is an undergraduate degree). When I graduated, I moved from the Gold Coast to Sydney to work for an accounting firm. I didn't become an accountant; I went into a niche, unloved specialty of the corporate finance world called "valuation consulting." We valued all kinds of things: first I valued private companies for couples who were divorcing, and later I valued more esoteric "assets"— damages in litigation cases, patents, and other so-called intangible assets. Although there are more senior women in accounting firms than there are senior leaders and PMs in investment management, there were still few female partners in the divisions where I worked: entrepreneurial services and corporate finance.

Unlike Ellen's more interesting romantic endeavors, mine were fairly boring. I was dating a guy who was offered the opportunity to work in the United States, and I agreed to follow him, so in that respect, we overlap by following a man, which is distressingly common. My job and life decisions led me from Sydney to Los Angeles and then to New York. As a consultant I worked in offices in different parts of the United States as well as in different countries. I also had the opportunity to travel internationally with my job; Italy, France, and the Philippines were some of the places I got to travel while working at Ernst & Young. As for the guy I followed across an ocean—we got married and had four kids, which makes me the boring one of our author pair. (Ellen's side note: Let's hear it for boring . . . I could have used a dose of that in my thirties.)

At the accounting firm, I valued things in hindsight—always looking in the rearview mirror. I wanted to move into the here and now and value things on a go-forward basis. I enrolled in a part-time MBA program at New York University's Stern School of Business. I digress here, but this is one area where I disagree with many full-time MBA students. A part-time MBA is tough, but it's a bargain, and in an era of rising tuition costs and resultant student debt, I highly recommend it. The degree you earn is the same as a full-time MBA degree, but often your firm will pick up some or all of the tuition tab, and you get paid a full-time salary at the same time. Sure, you miss out on all those side trips with your friends, but I had no debt exiting the program, and with a severely curtailed social life managed to save a little, too. Those savings have paid for many of my adventures later in life. From a practical perspective, doing a part-time MBA means that because you are working while studying, you get to put what you learn into practice immediately.

Getting back to my career trajectory . . . once I graduated, I took time to speak to a lot of people involved in the investment world. I had coffee with sell-side analysts, buy-side analysts, investor relations professionals, and investment bankers. I decided that I wanted to invest in businesses, and that is what led me to the buy side. Unlike Ellen, whose interviewing experience involved many interesting dinners and wine-lubricated conversations, I applied to a few jobs and then found an opening on the CFA Institute website. I got hired as a junior analyst at an IM firm. One of the reasons that I think I was able to skip the traditional sell-side job journey was that I had prior experience in valuation. The most important thing I learned at my first IM job was that you should be nice to your sell-side brokers—as that is how you might get your next job. After my firm restructured my position (which meant that I kept my job but was covering what I kindly referred to as "the crap of Europe"), through one of my sell-side friends I was offered the opportunity to interview at Franklin Mutual Series.

The interview at Mutual Series was similar to an MBA interview. You meet a bunch of people; if they agree that they could all work with you (our firm tends to choose four interviewers with distinct and diverse personalities), then you get asked back to make an investment pitch. The unknown secret in my pitch was that I used the Altman Z-score to analyze a business that had a bankruptcy risk—and Ed Altman, who developed it, was on the Mutual Series Fund board. This was the perfect example of the intersection of hard work and luck. I got hired on the spot.

Mutual Series is a unique place to work. Since I started there, and even before the rise of those pesky activist investors, we have been very vocal with companies about how we believe they can create long-term value for shareholders. We are not short-term investors; we think like the owners of these businesses. We actively engage with management, and we understand that real money is at stake. It's a unique process and one of the reasons that I love working at the company.

One of the things that distinguishes Franklin Mutual Series is how supportive it is of women. At the time I was hired, I was five months pregnant with my first daughter. It has been a great company to work for as I have transitioned from analyst to assistant portfolio manager to PM. I have had four children while working there, taking maternity leave for each of them but, by my own choice, continuing to maintain contact with the office with the support of some great colleagues. Working while having children with a working spouse (yes, my husband and I are balancers) was challenging at times, but we made it work. Yes, I have been pulled from meetings to deal with kid issues, but not often. And although the school nurse was still able to find only my contact information when issues arose, I had the ability to call on my husband to pitch in. Not only were there two of us to share these duties, we also had a support network that helped us.

I have had two mentor/sponsors at Mutual Series—both male—who have given me advice, nominated me for fellowships, and been a sounding board when things in my career weren't going well. They were also there when I needed to vent after having run into an egotistical male. In chapter 8 we told you that many of our interviewees found that having mentors and sponsors was invaluable—and I completely agree. Although I didn't have a female mentor, I did have a group of female peers to whom I turned throughout the years when I needed advice on how to deal with difficult situations, or if I just wanted advice on how to balance competing work and home life demands.

More Career Advice—Oh No!

My career developed during a period when many women were writing career advice books with conflicting and contradictory messages. I often found myself wondering if I should be leaning in or out, or whether I could have it all or some of it but not all the time. As a woman I was somewhat put off, because no one seemed to be telling men what to do. And this is why, when I am asked to give advice to women, I avoid providing a list of do's and don'ts. My personal journey, though a survey of only one, reflects the collective wisdom of someone who has done this for decades and has interacted with many successful PMs and analysts throughout her career. But it's not advice—it's the things I wish I'd known when I was a much younger version of me.

You Are Responsible for Your Career Development

Are you drifting along or taking proactive steps to manage your career? Step back and see if you are on track to reach your goals. Decide to move up, move over, or move on. Your career won't be a one-way shot to the stars—no one's is. There will be peaks and valleys. But you can't sit back and hope for promotions to come your way without making an effort on your own behalf. Don't accept repetitive projects that don't expand your knowledge and skill set, and make sure that the experience and knowledge you acquire as you go are relevant to where you want ultimately to be.

Setting your career on autopilot isn't the solution. You need to get into a zone where you are uncomfortable. No one told me to do a part-time MBA; I just realized that everyone else in senior positions at investment firms and on the sell side had one, so I enrolled in the program. I learned valuable lessons in leadership, management, operations, finance, and international business that have helped me in numerous ways in my portfolio management career.

Be Comfortable with Being Uncomfortable

We have talked about taking more career risk, and, yes, that can be uncomfortable—but that isn't what I wish I had learned early in my career. Rather, I wish I had known early on that being comfortable understanding that you will never know everything is an important career skill in IM.

As an analyst, you will have to make stock recommendations; sometimes you will have to make them quickly without complete information. For example, you thought a company was fabulous—and then out comes an announcement that there is an accounting error in how they booked supplier promotions. The stock is down 25 percent, and you will have to make a quick decision: (a) run for the doors—if they lied about the accounts, then they lied about other things; (b) hold—I don't have enough information and I need to talk to management; or (c) buy more—yes, they made a bad accounting decision, but the underlying fundamentals and cash flows of the business are still strong, and this represents the opportunity to buy into a great franchise at a fabulous 25 percent discount.

To be successful as a PM, as we have said before, you need to be able to give elevator pitches on stocks—you'll never know every detail of the investment case. So you have to trust that the analyst has done the work and that it is OK to know only the summary and offer to get back to someone who wants to dig further.

Aside from the analyst and PM roles, as you move from being a team member to a team leader in your organization, you'll also need to be comfortable with being uncomfortable. As a leader, you'll have to make decisions when not all the information is known. This is extremely important to learn as you go from being an analyst to a PM, and it is applicable across multiple fields as you move up the management leadership chain.

Be Nice to Everyone

The books might say that "nice girls don't get the corner office," but I haven't found that to be true. Be considerate of everyone, not just those above you. Not only is it the right thing to do, but I've seen many an administrative assistant who has helped make her boss's career.

Not being nice is a rookie mistake that I see way too often. Many people don't treat those working for them well. It is important to be appreciative of all the people in your organization, especially the administrative staff. That can pay off particularly when you find yourself in a bind. I was at dinner with a CEO who couldn't emphasize enough how important his assistant had been in helping him rise to the top—so much so that when he was asked to ring the opening bell at the NYSE, he had her up there on the podium with him.

Manage Up Better

When I started working at Mutual Series, I didn't take the time to get to know the senior managers and wish I had done better in that respect. It was easy to get the attention of my immediate boss (who sits next to me over a short partition), but what about my boss's boss, who is based in California? It is very important to make yourself known in your organization.

This is not about networking. Many women across industries are told that they need to do more networking. I believe that we actually do a good job at that—we just don't get the credit for it, and often we tend to like networking with people who look like us: other women, particularly women our own age.

Why is networking up so important? Working hard and going above and beyond are easy ways to get yourself noticed by the decision makers in your organization, and they are the ones who make promotion decisions. As we said earlier, it is your responsibility to manage your own career, and networking upward is an important component. You want to ensure that the first time the organization's decision makers hear your name isn't when they are considering you for a promotion.

Read, Read, and Read Some More

Reading helps you to think laterally. It helps you to look at the world as a puzzle and to look at things from a different perspective. It also makes for some interesting conversations. Read widely—from historical fiction to historical nonfiction, or corporate histories to beach reads. The average CEO reads a book a week; if they can make time for it, so can you.

I have always loved to read, but when I had children, reading fell by the wayside. I picked it up again about ten years ago, and these days I actively share book recommendations. I also like to give books as thank-you gifts. For example, a small group of female industrial investors and I formed an informal group called the "Iron Skirts," which hosts senior leaders from industrial companies for informal dinners. (You'll hear more about this group in chapter 11.) The idea is to learn from their career journeys and also, particularly for the female executives who attend, to provide them with advice on how to interact with Wall Street. As a follow-up, I might send one of our guests a book that I recently read to keep in touch and develop my network.

Join a Nonprofit Board

Joining a nonprofit board gives you the opportunity to expand your skill set. I am on the board of a nonprofit and the chair of our Audit Committee. I have learned a lot about audits, and that has helped me in unexpected ways as I interact with companies for my day job. You don't need to sit on a board; you can take a volunteer leadership role as well. Leadership in volunteer roles provides you with invaluable lessons on motivating and leading people.

Similarly, I encourage everyone to put her hand up to moderate and speak on panels and contribute outside the office. Let people know that you are willing to do this, so that when they are looking for people, your name comes to mind. But more important, when you take on these commitments, make sure you're prepared and bring your best self to the task. If you don't have the time to do it and do it well, then learn to say no.

Self-Care—Invest in Yourself; aka It's Ok to Watch The Real Housewives of Beverly Hills

I promised that I wouldn't give you any advice, and perhaps by venturing into this topic, I'm muddying the water. However, although this advice applies equally to men and women, it's something that I encounter more often with female peers and colleagues.

Women tend to put themselves at the bottom of the barrel. They prioritize working, taking care of the family, the house, the kids, and all the rest before taking care of themselves. But if you don't take care of yourself, you'll run yourself down. Call it "investing in me." Do something that makes you happy. It could be anything—watching *The Real Housewives of Beverly Hills*, going to a class at the local gym, or just walking in the park. Take care of you, because unless you take care of yourself, you won't be able to take care of anyone else.

What One Piece of Advice Do You Wish You Could Tell a 21-Year-Old Version of Yourself?

Speak up! No one can hear what you're thinking if you don't say it aloud.

Ellen's Path: Not Replicable Today . . . But Some Lessons Nonetheless

In chapter 5 I told you a bit about my path into IM, largely to point out that it couldn't have happened that way in today's super-competitive recruiting environment. In fact, many of my career steps were acci-dental—fortuitous parts of a random walk to a terrific career in IM. Although my story is something of an anachronism, some of the fac-tors in my success in IM are timeless, and I'll share these with you along the long, winding road from liberal arts major to PM.

In college I knew that a traditional corporate life wasn't for me. I watched one of my best (male) friends spend the better part of his senior year trying to get a job in investment banking, while other friends joined engineering, marketing, and consulting firms, and yet another group went to medical school. How I envied this last cohort—to know what you want to do from the day you enter college and to have your future mapped out. Today, if you want to work in IM out of college, you have to be in that special "knew it all along" group.

I didn't know what I wanted to do. I majored in literature, which meant I was good at, well, reading novels and writing about them. Not, you see, *writing* novels—an actual job—but writing *about* nov-els. I considered going for a literature graduate degree but intuited that that was not the right path for me. So I moved to New York City to live with my then-boyfriend, a writer for *Saturday Night Live* (this makes me sound much cooler than I was, or am), and spent two weeks looking for any entry-level job in publishing or public relations that I could find. When the opportunity to move to Los Angeles with the TV guy presented itself, I jumped at the opportunity. My banking friend suggested that I try consulting as a way of looking at different kinds of companies and jobs, and I secured a job at a tiny manage-ment consulting firm focused on the boring parts of the finance indus-try: insurance, savings and loans (remember S&Ls?), small banks.

I enjoyed the job, but things were not going well at home. My TV boyfriend, who made multiples above what I earned, ran off and left me for his production assistant, the cliché equivalent of the doctor leaving for his nurse. The day I saw them together was my Scarlett O'Hara nadir: as God was my witness, I would never depend on a man for money again. If I had had curtains in the tiny guesthouse that I downsized into after our breakup, I would have symbolically torn them into pieces, although likely would not have worn them. My taste ran more to Tahari.

My oracle banking friend had a new idea for me: business school. That would mean two years of my life, with a $50,000 price tag (more like $100k today), in exchange for, theoretically, the lucrative job of my dreams. Oh, and I might learn a few things, too. I took the GMAT, was stunned in a good way by my score—in no way predicted by my lackluster SAT score—applied to and got rejected from Stanford, cried for a minute, got into Kellogg, cried when I set foot in Evanston (I mean, have you ever? Don't), and spent the ensuing first year of B-school drinking and interviewing for a summer job on the sell side. By now I hope you know that means the Wall Street banks—Goldman, Morgan Stanley, JP Morgan, Bear Stearns, Deutsche Bank, Citi, Bank of America, Merrill Lynch, Lehman (yes, there is some nostalgia in running through this list)—and I met them all . . .

. . . at on-campus recruiting events, where a guy from Bear Stearns told us, "We buy our own rubber bands, so we take home the savings in our Bear Stearns stock!"—ultimately, worth nothing;

. . . in the pester-networking visits to their Chicago trading floors, where, I kid you not, I told an unimpressed Deutsche Bank managing director that every time I walked onto the trading floor, I got a rush. This was a lie, but it was what you were supposed to say;

. . . at dinners at Charlie Trotter's, where generally the best outcome was getting to sit next to one of my friends and drinking ourselves silly while lobbing in the occasional earnest question like, "What makes someone successful at Goldman Sachs?"—never Goldman, mind you. It took both words to convey the firm's significance.

I drank and networked my way through a summer in Morgan Stanley's fixed-income sales, trading, and research internship program. I emerged with two goals: I wanted to work on the buy side, which had to be kinder, gentler, and more intellectual than the sell side; and I wanted to get back to the West Coast—but this time on my own terms. Morgan Stanley introduced me to a client, Capital Group, and I was hired by one of the best companies in investment management.

Let's go back to chapter 5 for a minute to remind you how this could not happen today. From the moment I set my sights on that summer job on the sell side, by current standards I would have been pegged in recruiting as a sell-sider. Because I didn't work at Capital or any IM firm for my summer internship, I would have faced low odds of securing a buy-side job during second-year recruiting. And I never developed a stock pitch; twenty years ago, buy-side interviewing was more focused on cultural fit than the nuts and bolts of the job. At that time you weren't expected to know how to analyze securities; the idea was that you would develop an investing framework during your first few months at your analyst job.

I loved Capital. I loved the people, the work, and the money. But as I think about advice to young women entering the field of IM, it's hard not to boil it down to "try to get a job at Capital or a place like it." Capital has a terrific record of long-term results; it is one of few active investment managers that actually beats its benchmarks. People have written books about Capital, but that's not my intent here. Instead I'll try to distill what made me successful there—which might or might not be a recipe for success elsewhere.

Analyst Success: Read and Write Like a Literary Critic

I'll start by saying something provocative, if not controversial: everything I needed to know about investing I learned as a literature major. In college in the early 1990s, "lit crit" (literary criticism) was the cornerstone of all literary majors. I spent more time reading Derrida than de Maupassant; I knew Foucault rather than Fitzgerald. And in the course of all that tedious reading, I honed my critical analysis skills. When you apply a critical framework to a text, you engage in some of the most important components of security analysis.

- *Concise writing*: Remember how in freshman composition you learned about the components of a successful essay? Faulkner's "kill your darlings" advice works well in investing writeups. I am not sure what I think of an investment until I can distill my thesis into two or three concise sentences. One of the PMs who was an early fan of my work echoed Faulkner with his admonition to "edit, edit, edit" my protracted investment recommendations— and as I followed his advice, I found that the recommendations got better. A nice side effect of diligent writing is the paper trail, which keeps you honest. It's hard to say "I never liked Chesapeake" when your 2015 writeup sings the company's praises mere months before its bonds skidded into the $20s. Not that I bought Chesapeake then. Ok, I did.

- *Close reading*: Sometimes reading an annual report is like reading a novel. You have to remove yourself from other distractions and read closely to get the key themes of the piece, although of course you're looking for different things. In a novel, it's that poetic passage that stops you in your tracks to say, "How did Virginia Woolf *do* that?" In a company's annual report, poetry is a red flag—better that the company's team of writers and lawyers condense its narrative into clear, transparent prose.

- *Pattern recognition*: In the same way that I looked for literary influences in the texts I read in college (can you see Flaubert in de Maupassant? And don't even get me started on *Wide Sargasso Sea* or *The Hours* . . .), security analysis requires pattern recognition. How was the high-yield market in late 2015 like the one in 2002? Is the auto sector like the paging industry (rapid downward spiral) or like the wireline telecom business (melting ice cube)? As the COVID-19 pandemic accelerates the demise of the department store channel, will Macy's emerge as the sole survivor, or will its suppliers run for the hills à la Toys"R"Us? "I've been to this movie" are five of the most comforting words I murmur to myself, or another investor, when a company's trajectory changes.

You'll note that I have yet to mention quantitative skills. Consider them mentioned but demoted. Quantitative investing is its own world, and there are highly successful strategies in this almost entirely male universe. I'm not saying you can't build an amazing mathematical mousetrap to beat the market—just that it is by no means the only, or even the commonest, way to outperform. When you're analyzing companies and portfolios, most of what you need is basic math.

The "Hybrid" Years: Work–Work Balance (Analyst and PM Roles) While Trying to Create a Life to Balance

I wrote about my journey from analyst to PM in chapter 2, so I won't rehash it here. Becoming a PM was like my decision about having kids; I didn't think I'd ever want to be a PM until I did want to be a PM. Once that mental shift took place, I duly put up my hand. I had the benefit of working for a company that actually listened to me when I said I wanted to transition from analyst to PM. This transition started in 2006, and I kept part of my analyst day job as I built my PM record.

Those were long years of long hours, culminating in the toughest period of most investors' lives—late 2008 to early 2009. (Ask me again in a year or so if COVID-19 wins; the jury is out as of this writing.) I still had analyst coverage of the auto sector in addition to being a PM and spent long hours on calls with GMAC (renamed Ally) bondholder committees trying to piece together a government rescue plan that worked for everyone. I also put long hours into internal meetings encouraging PMs to sell GM bonds. I even got to speak to a couple of congressional committees about the auto companies. Oh, and meanwhile, another of my research holdings, General Growth Properties, went bankrupt. Plus, many bonds in my portfolio were trading at twenty cents on the dollar, and the private equity sponsors who sold them to us at par were trying to get us to crystallize those losses via distressed exchanges. (Don't ask.)

On the home front, I had decided in 2007 that I wanted to become a single mother. I had been married to my job for a decade by then, the silver lining of which was that I could afford fertility treatments, which were necessary because I had been married to my job, which meant I could afford fertility treatments, which were necessary because . . .

I'm sure you get my point about the circularity of all this. Fun times.

Lehman, Washington Mutual, and countless other more mundane bankruptcies later, we made it through the credit crisis. I had good results in 2008, and although I lagged the massive upturn in the market in 2009, that was a fairly typical return pattern that was easy to explain to clients. And then I went to a destination wedding in Lake Lure, North Carolina, and met my baby daddy. One "oops" baby later, I reluctantly decided to leave my job—which had been like my husband for more than a decade—and try being a stay-at-home mom, with time for all the things I couldn't do: philanthropy, trail running, yoga, writing . . . but soon I found I missed the markets.

The PM Years: You Can Have It All—The Job, I Mean

To reiterate a point we made early and often in this book, investment management is a fun job. Like that quote from *The Godfather*, I felt like I got pulled back in. A year after I decided not to go back to Capital after maternity leave, I took a job as a high-yield PM at a small firm. I began as a one-person high-yield shop, so I did everything— trading, research, and portfolio management. My PM job has shifted from relying on analysts' recommendations to construct my portfolios top down to building them bottom up with my own research. I truly believe that both models are workable in high-yield bond management, but it's difficult to explain to prospects how you can compete with the twenty-something people at Capital who make high yield happen there. (I'll share more about these challenges in chapter 12, which looks at the "allocators" of capital who listen to my pitch these days.)

I telecommute for this job, which gives me more flexibility to spend time with my son, and also to do all those things I wanted to do when I left Capital. My firm is supportive and deferential to my schedule, which is now complicated by joint custody.

My Insider Perspective on the Industry

In the course of working for a huge firm and a tiny one, I've come to a few conclusions about IM.

1. The cult of overwork and the image of the eighty-hour-a-week investor are myths. There are as many models for good investment results as there are for good portfolio managers—and there are far more models for mediocre results.

2. Although you might think that the resources of a bigger firm help its employees work fewer hours, bigger firms often fall into the meeting trap, which sucks up time without measurable benefits. Small firms can provide substantial flexibility because they remove the "arenas of display" (meetings) that drain the day of hours. Small firms can offer better work–life balance because they eliminate fake measures of performance and focus on actual performance.

3. The PM/analyst model can take many forms; it's not one size fits all.

4. Investment management *might* be headed toward a model like retail banking, with an oligopoly of a few huge firms (like my alma mater) providing services to the masses in fund structures, and a much larger number of small firms (like my current employer) providing customized service to institutional clients. But with technological and compliance costs marching ever higher, only the truly boutique, differentiated, service-focused small firms will survive—and they will have to stabilize fees to do so.

Ellen's Path, in Hindsight: Start at a Firm with an HR Department . . . Then Move to a Firm Without One

Remember the piece of advice to women in the prior chapter? "Go to work for a firm with an HR department if you want a fair shake." I think that's great advice for your first job in IM. But once you've built a track record, you might choose a different path; later in your career, you might want to go to work for a firm without an HR department. Many of us (including me) choose IM careers because we want to manage money, not people—and it's true that you don't have to manage people to make a great living in IM. But IM firms, like firms in many industries, tend to promote the people who are good at their jobs into management roles. And because big firms generously reward management types with stock, profit sharing, and other types of incentive compensation, being truly successful at many big firms means being part of management. If you just want to be left alone at your solitary Bloomberg terminal to analyze companies and build portfolios, sometimes a small firm is more comfortable.

Conclusion: We've Spent the Last Few Chapters Diagnosing the Problem—Let's Get to the Solutions!

We will end this chapter as we began it: by saying that we love our jobs, even though sometimes the market kicks our butts. We don't love that part. But like a marriage, a career in IM involves ups and downs and a commitment to riding out the latter because the good times are so much fun. Only one of us has been married (thus far), so this analogy might come across as disingenuous. But remember back to the constellation chapter and the perseverance comments from our interviewees. Although we have provided you with some best practices that have worked for us, there is no substitute in IM for grit. At the risk of sounding sexist, women are good at grit. (Hello, childbirth.)

Unfortunately, grit is not the only requirement—else there would be more female PMs. We will now move into our third and final section: a discussion of solutions to the industry's gender disparity.

PART THREE

Solutions to Investment Management's Gender Imbalance

Introduction

By this point in the book you've read about the industry's gender imbalance and the women who nevertheless made it to the top. But the most important part of our book lies ahead: the solutions. This section explores the changes (some already underway) required to increase the number of women who are interested in working in investment management and the number who are promoted to PM and, ultimately, management and board roles at IM firms. The structure mirrors prior sections, addressing solutions to the lack of female representation across the career spectrum, from getting more women in at the entry level (be it an undergraduate or a graduate) to keeping and promoting the talent that has already made it into the industry. The breadth of problems is reflected in the breadth of actions and solutions we profile in this section, although we doubt that our list is comprehensive. In fact, we know it isn't; some organizations declined to speak with us, and we are sure that we overlooked others.

A lot of smart women (sorry, guys, but the thought leaders on this topic are mostly women) have proposed solutions to the lack of diversity in different industries. We focus on IM, but many of our solutions are applicable to the broader finance industry as well as all of corporate America, particularly knowledge-based professions. A multifaceted approach to diversity in IM is necessary, which is why we are providing solutions at each point of the cycle that have resulted in a homogeneous IM landscape. Let's review the cycle that created our salient minority.

(a) Having few female senior leaders in an organization makes it difficult to recruit women (undergrads and MBAs) into the company, because they lack aspirational role models.

(b) Having fewer female recruits (entry-level analysts) creates a salient minority that depresses female retention rates, because the culture feels less friendly.

(c) Retaining fewer women means there are fewer women to promote to middle management (senior analysts and portfolio managers).

(d) Having fewer women in middle management begets fewer women in senior leadership roles.

(e) And the cycle repeats.

In order to increase the number of female PMs, solutions must focus on (a) recruiting more women into IM, (b) retaining these women once they are in the door, (c) promoting them to PM in a timely manner, and (d) addressing the lack of female leaders at IM firms and on their boards.

Throughout this book we have described PMs as the allocators of capital. However, later in this section we will introduce you to another industry participant: the entities that select the IM firms to invest their capital. As PMs, we allocate capital among companies that are listed on stock exchanges or have publicly traded bonds. However, this is not *our* money; it belongs ultimately to pension funds, endowments, and family offices—a group broadly referred to in our industry as "allocators." These allocators are sometimes advised by consultants, who assist them in selecting investment managers. We have devoted an entire chapter to these important players, who play a role in moving the needle on the abysmal 1 percent of money that is managed by firms that are majority owned by women.

We'll go back to a quote from our prologue: "Ginger Rogers had to do everything Fred Astaire did—but in heels, backwards." We want the next generation of women in investment management to move forward, in flats, just as our male peers do. And we are lobbying for this even though it means giving up the perks of being a salient minority (we say this only partly tongue in cheek). Sure, there are no lines in the women's bathrooms at conferences. And although we stand out in a sea of gray suits or Patagonia bro-vests when meeting a company CEO—which can make our questions more memorable or get us the call back from the IR person—we would much prefer to see a more gender-balanced room of investors.

From our interviews, discussions with students, and cocktail sessions with colleagues, we've found that lots of women are bypassing flats and are already in sneakers. These women can't wait to groan at the sight of the bathroom line. And although we're not rushing out to buy those hideous bro-vests, we are forging our own path toward solutions to make our profession homogeneous.

10

Solutions—Widening the IM On-Ramp

As promised, we'll propose solutions along the IM career path, and here we begin with the pipeline in colleges and business schools. This chapter came easily to us after our review of the undergraduate and graduate survey data and lots of conversations (both in-person and virtual) with young women across the pipeline, from new college students to second-year MBAs with job offers in IM. A lot of it will sound familiar, as it involves fixing the deficiencies in career awareness and recruiting processes that we highlighted in chapters 4 and 5. It also might sound obvious—but it will require commitment from universities and IM firms, as well as partnerships with organizations that were created to improve our industry's gender balance. We'll introduce you to some of these, and their passionate founders, in the pages to come.

Recruiting More Women Into IM

Like IM, recruiting is a numbers game. We recommend the following changes to the existing recruiting process:

(a) Increase the visibility of the IM career;

(b) address IM's image problem;

(c) provide more on-ramps to a career in IM;

(d) improve women's investment literacy (as distinct from financial literacy);

(e) change the recruiting criteria; and

(f) support organizations that focus on improving the pipeline.

Increase the Visibility of the IM Career

As Marian Wright Edelman, founder of the Children's Defense Fund, puts it succinctly: "You can't be what you can't see." We all know who Warren Buffett is, but before you read our constellation chapter, you might not have been able to invoke the names of any female investors. We're not the only ones working on this visibility issue. Bloomberg's New Voices Program, of which one of your authors is part, focuses on "diversifying newsroom sources."[1]

100 Women in Finance, another firm working to increase the profile of female PMs, recently launched a female PM visibility campaign.[2] Founded two decades ago by three women who worked in the hedge fund industry, the organization was originally called "100 Women in Hedge Funds"—an aspirational goal in a male-dominated industry. Since tactically changing its name, the organization has hosted educational and networking events for its membership (which includes your coauthors) and supports the next generation of women through mentorships and other opportunities. Conferences and events showcase *women*. "Our panels typically feature women as the investment experts, a refreshing alternative to standard finance industry gatherings," says CEO Amanda Pullinger. One recent initiative focused on increasing the visibility of female PMs, engaging more of them to be keynote speakers at other industry events. 100 Women in Finance has also focused on increasing diversity in the pipeline, partnering with industry participants to

host dinners so that female high school students can hear from successful women in finance.

The best place to provide visibility for any professional career is in the career management centers (CMCs) of colleges and MBA programs. At the MBA level, CMCs have come a long way since we graduated from business school decades ago. They host women-only networking events with IM firms, information sessions about the career, and intensive pitch reviews, among other things. Our sense is that at the college level, improving exposure to IM is still a work in progress; although a few IM firms, such as Oaktree and Capital Group, have targeted IM recruiting programs at the undergrad level, the paucity of truly entry-level jobs in IM suggests that IM career awareness building needs to come from elsewhere.

Address IM's Image Problem

Let's say that our awareness initiatives are successful, and we've attracted a group of stellar young women to interview. We're about to hit another roadblock: Gordon Gekko. Houston, we have an IM image problem. We believe the problem can be addressed by focusing on our role as stewards of capital, highlighting the growth of ESG and impact investing, and generally showcasing the positive side of what we do. We also need to recast activist investors (when appropriate!); they're not necessarily the bad guys attacking Chipotle but, rather, the good guys helping lost companies find their way through better capital allocation, better execution of their strategy, and better management.

We admit that this call to arms is somewhat out of our control, but nonetheless we direct it to Hollywood, the book publishing industry, and the news media: talk about the good aspects of our industry alongside its (well-covered) deficits. We're not asking for untruths or even half-truths—just balance. The umpteenth story about the overpaid hedge fund manager who put millions in the bank while his clients lost everything is an attention-grabbing headline, but it overstates the prevalence of these bad actors and renders invisible the vast majority of us who are just trying to help our clients retire comfortably. Here's a thought: a screenplay for "The Lehman Sisters" movie—a fictionalized account of what the financial crisis would have looked like had women been running the world's largest financial institutions in 2008. Surely if people will pay Broadway prices to sit through three and a half hours of *The Lehman Trilogy*, they'd watch this mercifully briefer show on the big screen.

We'll make one other observation—and recommendation—before leaving this topic. Men in our industry are unapologetic about what they do; they tend to highlight the importance of their jobs to the finance ecosystem. Women are less proud to say they are PMs working in finance. As a former student working in distressed debt (one of the most "vulturistic" asset classes) said, "I don't think of it as grave-dancing at all. These companies need help restructuring and running their businesses better, and that's what we do." At the risk of overgeneralizing, we find a lot more of our female than male peers making apologies for their jobs. We need to stop downplaying the good we can do for our clients by investing their money successfully. We need to extoll the virtues of what we are doing for our clients; by investing their money prudently in assets that generate index-beating returns, we can make the difference between a kid whose parents can afford to send her to college and one who graduates with a boatload of debt. We should beat our chests proudly when asked what we do rather than muttering into our wine glasses.

Provide On-Ramps to an IM Career

In response to the overwhelmed, stretched college CMCs, third-party organizations have leapt into the gap to focus specifically on introducing young women to the IM career and helping them into the pipeline. Pathways Programs incorporate the benefits of mentoring and student clubs, as well as giving students an advantage in securing internships. Additionally, through the connections and sponsors of these programs, students are more likely to secure desirable internships, getting hands-on experience and real-time understanding of life in the investment management profession. Another benefit of these programs is that the students begin to build their own peer networks. Many students in these programs continue to be connected, through friendships and other professional networks, well after the program is over. Other programs, such as Road to Wall Street, educate women about the skills needed to succeed in IM and introduce them to investment professionals through guest speakers and formal mentoring programs.

Girls Who Invest (GWI)[3] is one of the best known of the on-ramping programs aimed at college women. It was founded by Seema Hingorani in response to her experience as chief investment officer at the New York City Employees' Retirement System. She was responsible for allocating $160 billion of pension money to investment firms—and all she saw on organizational charts was a sea of white men on investment teams. When she asked the IM firms about this, they said they lacked a pipeline of women entering the profession. Hingorani set out to change that.

GWI recruits university students into its intensive flagship summer training program, which is followed by paid internships at established IM firms—including the firm that employs one of your authors, who sponsors a GWI intern and speaks during the educational part of the overall program. In the training program the young women gain valuable skills that will help them excel in their internships, and the employers avoid the time and expense of training each intern. In addition to valuable training, GWI addresses another issue: the lack of female peer networks. GWI creates one with every summer class.

A different take on college on-ramping is represented by Phelps Forward (PF),[4] which helps first-generation college women and graduates find internships and full-time jobs at finance firms, including IM firms. PF has two career development programs: a three-year program for women looking to go into financial services in finance or tech roles, and an ongoing program for graduates who are already working in financial services.

PF founder Alicia Ames explains,

> Many top colleges are not able to help these women find the great jobs they could get if they were fully aware of the opportunities available to them, and prepared for them. They often know nothing about the finance industry before applying to PF, despite being very educated. They are sometimes intimidated and don't think they are qualified before they apply to the program. They want to be as prepared as possible for their jobs, though, and they don't want to oversell themselves. Due to the preparation they receive in the program, they do extremely well in securing positions with top finance firms, setting off on a very successful career trajectory. This is such an important achievement for them, and often the fulfillment of both their dreams and their families' many dreams—as well as decades of hard work from all of them to get to that point.

We hope that Ames's comments sound familiar—they echo some of the themes from chapters 4 and 5 about the challenges for women undergrad and graduate students who are in pursuit of IM careers. PF has fifteen corporate partners and counting, including marquis firms such as Oaktree, DoubleLine, Loomis Sayles, Alliance Bernstein, and JP Morgan, all of which are extremely pleased with the performance of PF scholars on the job.

Where GWI and PF focus on college students, the WIN (Women in Investing) Conference at Cornell University's Parker Center for Investment Research is Cornell's effort to educate, connect, and place more women in IM at both the undergraduate and MBA levels. Started in 2010, the MBA conference arose from founder and Executive Director Lakshmi Bhojraj's observation that the business school's student-managed fund, like the industry overall, had a significant gender imbalance (usually about five women out of twenty-five to thirty students)—and that the number wasn't moving much.

WIN created a forum for interested MBA students and successful women from IM firms. The conference includes a mix of formats to maximize learning and networking opportunities:

- "How-to" panel sessions (research a company, generate investment ideas, etc.)
- A stock pitch (the students select their own stock to pitch) judged by professionals
- Interviews with sponsor companies
- Speed-networking sessions
- A detailed look at career paths in the industry

The participants from the sponsor firms by and large are female, but WIN is not for women only; men from sponsor firms are also encouraged to attend. Since its inception, WIN has hosted 575 female MBA students from twenty-one schools. Today it has twenty sponsor companies (it started with eight). Of its alumnae, 45 percent are working in IM and enjoy a ready-made network of all past participants.

WIN is a terrific event for the many MBA programs that send women to participate, and it showcases talent that is typically already on a finance or IM path in business school. (Recall our discussion about the need to hit the ground running for first-year MBA recruiting in chapter 5.) To reach students earlier in their careers, Cornell has also started hosting the Undergraduate WIN Conference (which some alumnae and sponsors refer to as "Baby WIN"). According to Bhojraj, "Undergrads have a harder time finding out about careers in IM because companies don't do a lot of marketing or on-campus recruiting at the undergrad level. We opened up the event to students as early as sophomore year to make sure we reach women early enough." Undergrad WIN hosts 60–65 students per year from fourteen schools and is growing. There is some overlap with the WIN sponsor firms but also a different set of participants (such as firms like AQR Capital Management, a quantitative investment firm, and Dimensional Fund Advisors), which are looking for something a bit different from the traditional stock pitch.

We applaud GWI, PF, Cornell, and (we hope!) other programs in the wings that encourage and enable young women to join us. Although the jury is out on these programs as their graduates work their way through the promotion pipeline, from analyst to PM to management, the early data is promising.

Improve Women's Investment Literacy: Teach Stock and Bond Market Literacy and Basic Investing Concepts

High school is ground zero for remedying the lack of gender diversity in investment management. Although we have downplayed the role of math in earlier chapters, there's no question that the math skills students begin developing well before college are an essential building block of investing acumen. In its study of diversity in IM, the CFA Institute recommended that the industry focus on "building math and technical skills . . . even earlier [than college]."[5] A UNESCO report found that only 35 percent of global STEM students in higher education are female.[6] Encouraging more high school girls to study math is an important and necessary step toward increasing the pipeline of women in IM.

At the risk of stating the obvious, exposure to the basics of investing can only help to raise IM's visibility as a career option. But there's a wide range of financially related offerings in high schools, and they tend to be more prevalent in higher socioeconomic areas. Title 1 schools have the greatest need and the fewest resources to run these programs. It is up to us as finance professionals to show up as volunteers, role models, and advocates for these girls.

We have deliberately not referred to this type of offering as financial literacy, which tends to focus on budgeting for the household and opening bank accounts. Though these are vital topics, we also need to teach market-relevant topics, such as becoming familiar with the differences among stocks, bonds, real estate, and other types of investments. The skills learned in these classrooms are advantageous for everyone, regardless of gender. That said, women seem to be at a greater disadvantage when it comes to obtaining this knowledge, creating a wealth gap as they get older. Making these types of courses mandatory could provide visibility for IM at a very early stage in career exploration. One student told us that the activities in her high school class led her to pursue finance:

> In my high school business class, we learned the basics of financial accounting and did a stock trading simulation. I was really good at it and enjoyed doing it. After that, I started reading up on markets and reading quarterly earnings reports. That class really inspired me to become interested in the markets and a potential career in investing.

Rock the Street, Wall Street (RTSWS), a nonprofit founded by Maura Cunningham, is a financial and investment literacy program designed to spark the interest of a diverse population of girls into entering careers in finance. RTSWS has chapters in thirty-three high schools in seventeen U.S. cities, with plans to grow its footprint. As compared with a financial literacy program that focuses on budgeting and managing daily living expenses, RTSWS assigns hands-on investment projects to high school girls. These students learn about capital markets—stocks, bonds, and investments in general. According to founder Cunningham, RTSWS students experience a 92 percent increase in financial and investment literacy (that's a running three-year average), and its alumnae are four times more likely than female students in the national population to pursue degrees in finance, economics, or a related field.

Cunningham believes—and we agree!—that the industry needs more of these programs to reach girls at a pivotal time in their lives—before entering college, when they are deciding if and where they're going to go to school and what they are going to study. Local CFA societies, 100 Women in Finance, and major IM firms including JP Morgan, Blackrock, Alliance Bernstein, and Invesco are partnering with RTSWS to reach and cultivate these future career candidates at earlier ages.

Change the Recruiting Criteria: De-Bias the Entry-Level Recruiting Process

Books have been written about flawed recruiting processes across corporate America. With respect to IM specifically, you might remember some of the MBA recruiting stories from chapter 5. Although biased recruiting practices are by no means limited to IM, they have a magnified impact there. Our aim in this section is to propose some concrete steps that IM-focused recruiters can take to mitigate both conscious and unconscious bias against women. By the way, we're not just talking to actual recruiters and HR folks here. Considering that IM candidates are typically exposed to a dozen or more PMs and analysts in the interview process, these prescriptions are aimed at the large number of practitioners who contribute to hiring decisions.

Routinize the process. As PF founder Alicia Ames told us,

> If I could change anything about the recruiting process throughout the industry, it would be to routinize it and make it much more transparent in advance, so all candidates knew what they needed to learn long before that moment. When the process isn't transparent, it's much easier to keep hiring homogeneous candidates, especially from higher income levels, as they have more inside knowledge.

At the college level, interviews run the gamut from rigorous analytical tests to chatty "getting to know you" experiences. Ames says,

You can have one candidate who interviews with a senior executive who really wants to get to know her personality, her capabilities, and long-term value, who isn't asking a lot of detailed technical questions, and a different candidate interviewing with a twenty-two-year-old analyst just out of college who wants to do a very intense technical interview and may not really understand the benefit of hiring someone very different from them.

Ames's recommendations (and ours) are that IM firms provide interview training that focuses on standardized criteria, and that they review interviews to ensure that the process is consistent and thorough.

Conduct joint evaluations. At the entry-level interview stage, joint evaluation is an important tool to counter gender bias. Evaluators rely less on the cognitive shortcuts that allow gender bias to creep into the selection process when they evaluate more than one candidate at once. The mere presence of those other comparatives means that the comparison set and calibration are easier, and it also highlights "the trade-offs between what people *want* and what they *should do*."[7] In lay terms, this means that if a candidate is evaluated individually, to make things easy on the interviewer, that person will make stereotypical assessments of what he or she expects based on the candidate's gender or other observable factors. This introduces unconscious bias into the decision-making process. When the interviewer is required to evaluate a candidate as a member of a pool, the comparison effects overcome the interviewer's unconscious bias.

Incidentally, joint evaluation is a critical tool in investing as well. A PM would never make an investment in a vacuum; comparing a company with its peers as well as other investment opportunities is a key part of the decision process.

De-lionize investing experience—and the stock pitch. We highlighted this in chapters 4 and 5. Lots of folks in our industry are suckers for the story about the kid who saw his friends playing a brand new video game and bought Electronic Arts, or the one who used his mom's new wardrobe choices as a basis for buying Lululemon stock. Recruiters need to wean themselves off asking for these stories as they favor rich white males, for two reasons:

- There is a well-documented tendency for parents to talk more to sons than to daughters about finance and investing.
- Although our book is about the lack of gender diversity in investment management, these recruiting practices are also biased against candidates—both men and women—from less privileged backgrounds.

Our MBA chapter highlighted how many IM interviews are held during the early part of one's MBA—that is, before you've learned all the skills you need to do the job. We know from a Hewlett Packard study that if women don't meet 100 percent of the job requirements, they are less likely to apply for a position than a man who only meets 60 percent of them.[8] A woman who has limited experience with stock picking is unlikely to apply for an IM position before she has taken the requisite MBA finance class, by which time she might have completely missed the first round of IM recruiting. We also question the necessity of doing a stock market pitch at all as part of the IM hiring process, given its potential to discourage women from applying. What other profession requires you to know how to do the job before you're hired?

Do We Attempt "Blind" Interviews? We Don't Think So

Various studies have shown that the only way to eliminate bias completely is to blind recruiters completely. For example, in an orchestra setting, the use of curtains to mask gender from an evaluator resulted in a significant increase in the number of women hired.[9] Would a similar approach work in IM? We are skeptical. Although you can eliminate names from résumés, we found a number of countervailing forces at work.

- Many investment managers are actively looking for female analysts and PMs. Eliminating indicative gender details at a time when it could actually help women is counterproductive.
- Eliminating all gender indicators sounds great in theory but is difficult to do in practice.
- This industry, particularly at the senior level, involves a lot of networking. It's hard to get anything other than an entry-level job without an introduction. As one of our midcareer interviewees told us, "Every single job I've gotten has been through someone I worked with."

Conclusion

There are a lot of ways to engage young women earlier in the IM recruiting process. For the young women who should be considering the field along with the more typical paths to medicine and law, this largely boils down to exposure—to women who do the job, the job description, and the language and skills they need to jump through the interview hoops. But it's not all up to the girls. The IM firms looking for these young women must de-bias their recruiting and hiring processes, which are structured to find investing prodigies (which we argue are optical illusions) at the expense of diversity and raw talent.

In our next chapter we'll imagine a world in which females match males in a starting "class" of investment analysts—and provide a retention roadmap for the IM firms that spend time, money, and energy recruiting them.

11

Solutions—Retaining and Promoting Women in IM

Great news: we followed the directives in the prior chapter, and our recruiting efforts worked. We have a gender-balanced incoming class of new analysts. But as you saw in earlier chapters, this isn't translating into better gender diversity. Why? Although retention is an issue for many businesses, IM has a particularly bad track record of retaining women. A Citigroup report found that the financial industry saw an average 23 percent decline in women between the junior and management levels from 2014 to 2017 (only health care and real estate were worse).[1] If we are to be successful in getting women through the front doors of IM firms, what can we, as an industry, do to put these bright new analysts onto the PM path, promote them into senior leadership roles, and, ultimately, get them into the boardroom?

There's a black cloud on the horizon for those bright new female analysts. Even though an increasing number of managers in IM acknowledge that improving diversity and inclusion can improve performance, it can be difficult to convince employees of the benefits of diversity. Margaret Neale of Stanford University found that

when newcomers were socially similar to the team, old team members reported the highest level of *subjective* satisfaction with the group's productivity. However, when *objective* standards were measured, they performed the worst on a group problem-solving task. When newcomers were different [from the existing team], the reverse was true. Old members thought the team performed badly, but in fact it accomplished its task much better than the homogeneous group.[2]

When a diverse person (i.e., a female) joins a homogeneous team (of white men), she might improve performance, but her team members might not acknowledge or be aware of her contribution.

As much as we love the idea of radical change in our workforce, we acknowledge the shortcomings of a rules-based approach to gender diversity, which Neale and others have encountered in their studies. A "command and control" attitude won't produce lasting behavioral change. A message from the top that "your department needs to get to gender parity by 2025" can alienate (male) managers. It's demotivating to hear "hire X% more women," with the implied follow-on, "or else you will be replaced, the company could be sued, or both." Although "sticks" like aggressive, quantitative diversity targets can achieve short-term solutions, we prefer "carrot" approaches that identify and increase awareness of the problem, outline the quantifiable benefits of gender diversity, and give managers the tools to get to gender parity.

We know this is possible because there are precedents—or, to use a term that industry practitioners will find comfortable, "benchmarks." For example, in 1999, the Massachusetts Institute of Technology discovered that it had unintentionally discriminated against women. How did it figure this out? By examining data on salary, space, awards, and responses to outside offers. The data showed that at critical points in their careers, men were getting access to more resources than were women. As one of the deans at the time said, "It was data-driven, and that's a very MIT thing."[3] Using this data, MIT made changes that led to a near doubling of its female faculty and the promotion of several women into senior leadership positions over the ensuing decade.[4] This is a roadmap of the change we would like to see in IM: data driven; evolutionary, not revolutionary; and meaningful over a reasonable time frame.

Using MIT and other benchmarks as touchstones, in this chapter we will provide a roadmap for IM firms to improve gender diversity. We have not reinvented any wheels; the solutions in the pages that follow draw from a large body of research. Our own reading list is much more exhaustive, but we have attempted to condense what we've learned about countering gender bias in the workplace into a concrete action list. You'll find a lot of versions of the phrase "studies show" in the pages that follow—which is good news. There are, in fact, lots of tested, validated solutions to IM's woman problem.

Our list of solutions falls into three categories, which overlap in some areas.

1. Equalize promotion
   a. Mine data for gendered trends in promotions.
   b. Reform evaluation criteria to reduce (dare we say, eliminate!) bias against women.
   c. Introduce an evaluation nudge.
   d. Address the promotion delay.
   e. Identify leaks in the pipeline.
   f. Increase women's representation at *all* levels—PMs, senior leadership, and the boardroom.
2. Equalize pay
   a. Mine data for gendered trends in pay.
   b. Provide more pay transparency.
3. Equalize culture
   a. Create advocates and allies.
   b. Invest in the *right* diversity and inclusion training to combat rather than reinforce bias.
   c. Provide counseling to managers.
   d. Mentor and sponsor women.
   e. Provide networking opportunities.
   f. Purge most artifacts of the "bro culture"; leaven some with female alternatives.

Let's Start with the Data

IM is an industry awash in data. Analysts crunch numbers provided by companies, statistical databases, and hundreds of other data sources. PMs analyze their portfolios six (ok, more) ways to Sunday: exposures, risk weightings, shock scenarios, attribution. . . . We live and breathe data, but when it comes to analyzing ourselves, we can be like the proverbial barefoot children of cobblers. We are not unique in this respect; only 42 percent of organizations review performance evaluations according to gender to identify disparities.[5] But considering that we are, arguably, uniquely good at data analysis, we should be at the forefront of using data to identify our biases. As data becomes increasingly available, companies will be unable to hide by using excuses such as "we didn't know" or "it's a pipeline issue," because by doing so, they risk having their own data analyzed by an outside expert—who shows clearly what the company is missing.

Equalize Promotion: What Is Our Data Wish List?

It's no secret that women aren't afforded as many sponsorship and promotion opportunities as their male colleagues. McKinsey found that for every hundred men promoted to manager, only seventy-nine women are promoted.[6] In chapter 3 we shared CFA Institute data showing that 14 percent of analysts are female, versus the Morningstar study that led to our writing this book showing only 10 percent of PMs are female.[7] Since the analyst-to-PM transition is widely viewed as a promotion, these statistics highlight a gender promotion gap roughly in line with that shown in the McKinsey study.

With respect to promotion, we'll start with some statistics jargon. IM firms should ensure that their performance ratings follow a standard normal distribution; that the distribution is equivalent in terms of its mean and standard deviation for the female and male members of each of their divisions and experience levels; and that they are equivalent for both the female and the male members of your division. This is a long-winded way of saying that firms should make sure that women and men are treated equally in performance evaluations. The best way to do this is with data mining and tracking. The list below is by no means exhaustive, but we recommend tracking the following data within IM firms:

- analyst track records to ascertain whether there is a difference between the performance of male analysts' recommendations compared with those of women;
- the amount of time that women spend as analysts before being promoted to senior analyst or PM compared with their male colleagues;
- the impact of industry assignments on promotion to PM—and whether there are consistently gender-oriented industry assignments (recall our discussion of "low value seats" in chapter 6);
- the representation of women in revenue-generating positions compared with their representation in administrative positions;
- senior leadership and board member gender composition;
- if applicable, the number of women sent on international assignments compared with the number of men (international assignments at multinational companies are often viewed as necessary steps to senior leadership roles);
- male versus female PM performance, with appropriate adjustments for any differences in asset class, sector, etc.; and
- the gender composition of employees who are sent to executive training programs.

Tracking these metrics should reveal gendered trends in promotion. With this data in hand, organizations can utilize the approaches we outline next to improve women's promotion outcomes.

Reform Evaluation Criteria and Feedback

Researchers have found that some performance evaluation criteria encourage bias in evaluation.[8] Additionally, women are more likely to be provided with nonspecific feedback, whereas men are provided with more concrete advice. When the criteria are not clear or the context is ambiguous, bias is more prevalent. And for women looking to improve their chances of promotion, nebulous, unclear advice is unhelpful, absent mind-reading. The solution is to restructure performance evaluation criteria and feedback to make them gender-neutral, standardized, and consistently applied. Enhanced performance criteria should adjust for potential bias as well as for male overconfidence.

Objectively evaluating teams and their members, and making those results visible, is likely to benefit the entire organization. Although quantitative performance—how your portfolio performs—is easy to observe, evaluating soft skills is harder. Fortunately, a growing number of organizations are developing strategies to help with this; for example, LinkedIn's Global Talent Trends Report 2019 describes new tools to help firms evaluate these skills objectively.[9]

One final suggestion is to incorporate reviewer accountability into performance criteria. Put managers on notice that they must provide concrete examples to support promotion recommendations and that they'll be called on to explain consistently higher ratings for males than for females.

The "Evaluation Nudge"

Researchers Bohnet, van Geen, and Bazerman came up with the concept of an "evaluation nudge," a method of performance evaluation to counter gender bias.[10] Similar to the joint evaluation tool discussed in the prior chapter, the nudge suggests that employees be evaluated jointly rather than individually to eliminate gender stereotypes and focus on individual performance.

Why does this system work? As discussed in the interviewing process, when you evaluate a single candidate, your only reference point is something that you have experienced or a stereotype that you hold. When you evaluate two candidates, your reference point becomes the other candidate. Bohnet et al.'s research found that in separate evaluations, 51 percent of employers chose the underperforming candidate (a lower-performing male versus a higher-performing female), but when these two candidates were evaluated jointly, only 8 percent chose the underperforming employee—whereas 92 percent chose the higher-performing employee.

One limitation of the Bohnet et al. study is that it looked at so-called marginal candidates when the hiring decision was a close call. Although all of us in finance likely think that we are above average (similar to how drivers rank their driving skills), we believe that the individual performance evaluation is referenced against the average finance candidate score, so the results should be equally applicable.

Address the Promotion Delay

The CEO of Salesforce.com acknowledged that his company promoted a man in twenty-four months but promoted a woman in thirty-six months. Why this happens is hard to determine exactly. Could it be that women ask for a promotion only when they have 100 percent of the skills they need to move to the next level, whereas men put their hands up when they are 60 percent qualified? Or is it because women start self-selecting out of challenging new roles when they are thinking about having children? Or do women ask questions about a job that male managers take to mean "no" rather than "tell me more"? You'll never find out unless you track the data and ensure that women's career trajectories mirror those of their male counterparts.

Identify the "Leaks" in Your Internal PM Pipeline

Remember Tanya from chapter 6? She was the diligent analyst who should have been promoted to PM but left instead. There are many Tanya stories in IM—including women who leave after having kids, women who leave after being given their umpteenth Brussels sprouts industry to cover, and women who get subtly pushed out for being "too aggressive." IM firms need to use data to identify leaks in their PM pipelines. Given that women leave at any of several pressure points, it is crucial to design programs that are targeted at each part of the PM pipeline.

The term "affirmative action" can raise hackles for both women and men, as some view it as synonymous with "advancement without merit." Rather than view the next three suggestions to IM firms in that light, we would reframe them as opportunities for IM firms to give women a nudge to improve female retention. This might sound deliberately provocative, but our intent is not to punish males with good results. Rather, we want to ensure that females with good performance are considered for all promotion opportunities even if theirs aren't the loudest voices in the room.

a. When consolidating funds and eliminating PM positions, eliminate male PMs rather than female PMs. This reduces the denominator—and pushes the female percentage up.

b. Promote female analysts to PM over male analysts. This increases both the numerator and the denominator—and pushes the female percentage up.

c. Replace departing male PMs with qualified female PMs who have demonstrably good track records. This increases the numerator—and pushes the female percentage up.

Create Female Senior Leaders

The lack of females at the highest levels has a mouthful of a name: "vertical gender occupational segregation." At the risk of stating the obvious, we don't just need more females in PM roles; we need them in other senior leadership roles in IM and as board members. Your authors skew positively in this respect: we both work for firms with female CEOs. But we are the exception, and it's also worth pointing out that we were both promoted to PM under male CEOs.

According to a McKinsey study, "finance has a steep drop-off in female representation between entry and middle-management roles."[11] As this is the pipeline into senior management, it follows that we are underrepresented in those ranks as well. Addressing the lack of female IM leaders needs to occur at the C-suite level, at the board level, and at the firm founder level. We will discuss the first two of these in this chapter and return to the founder issue in the next chapter.

Invest in Career Counseling

In chapter 6 we discussed women's tendency (relative to men) to underinvest in networking—to the detriment of their career progression. Making it into a PM role is hard, but at least it has some tangible performance metrics to support women's journeys. Unfortunately, the attributes that lead to senior leadership roles are much less tangible, and we have shown in umpteen different ways that unclear promotional criteria can discriminate against women.

We believe that part of the solution is career counseling for female employees, which can provide them with concrete actions and a promotion plan in their rise to leadership positions. Many women would love an action plan—and third-party career counselors are well suited to providing plans. Investing in rising female employees can increase the representation of women within both the company and its leadership ranks.

Put More Women in the Boardroom, Already!

Goldman Sachs was recently celebrated for declaring that it would not manage initial public offerings (IPOs) for companies without female representation on their boards of directors. Although we would point out that Goldman, and other investment banks, make a lot more fees on secondary equity and bond offerings than they do on IPOs, we applaud this philosophy. Goldman practices what it preaches; its board is one quarter female. There is also a California law that requires that every public company in the state have at least one female board member. (This is somewhat limited in impact, as most companies, regardless of their headquarters location, choose to register as Delaware corporations for legal reasons.)

Board gender diversity has improved as the result of these and other initiatives, along with pressure from large institutional shareholders like Blackrock, but it is still a long way from parity. Board diversity begets diversity outside the boardroom; a 2017 MSCI study found that the more women there were on a company's board of directors, the more women there were in senior leadership and throughout the company.[12] How many directors does it take to make a difference? MSCI found that even one or two female directors correlated with a meaningfully higher percentage of senior female leaders. This correlation between female board members, female leadership, and female workforce quantifies the obvious: women prefer to work at companies where role models of their own gender provide clear evidence of a career path.

In IM there are two types of boards: the traditional board of directors of the IM firm itself, and mutual fund boards. (Each SEC-registered mutual fund has its own board of directors.) Board representation at listed IM firms is about 25 percent female,[13] which is slightly better than the 20 percent average for corporate America.[14] The numbers look similar for mutual fund boards: 28 percent of fund board members are female.[15] As Blackrock (whose board is 28 percent female) pushes its portfolio companies for better board gender diversity, it and its peers need to look in the mirror.

A Credit Suisse study on gender diversity provides the following (perhaps obvious) ways for firms to change board composition:

a. Replace male directors with female directors with no change in the size of the board.
b. Add a female director by enlarging the size of the board.
c. Remove a male director from a board. Although this helps arithmetically (as long as there is at least one female board member), it is our least preferred option, because it doesn't increase diversity of thought in the boardroom.

There are always naysayers when the concept of diversity for its own sake comes up. As it relates to the boardroom, here's a thought. We discussed in earlier chapters the tendency of women to overprepare for meetings—and their behavior is similar in the boardroom. An AMP Capital study[16] found that male directors observed that female directors were more likely to have read the board papers in more detail. What happened next? The men started reading them in more detail, too. Better-prepared board members, longer discussions, and more robust discussions of key issues—the benefits of increasing diversity in the boardroom accrue not just to the company but to other male directors as well. Just think about the lower liability they will have for potentially negligent actions.

Equalize Pay

Research on the pay disparity between men and women—even equally qualified men and women—is voluminous. Our industry, despite its legendary compensation, doesn't look different based on the small number of studies that have been done. One recent survey of bonuses in the long-only and hedge fund industry found that we, too, have a pay gap with our male colleagues—women bonuses for PMs and senior analysts are 30 percent lower than for their male counterparts.[17] Without rehashing data you've doubtless seen before, we will simply lament that women make, on average, 80 percent of the wages of men, while we also list a number of compounding factors.

1. *The motherhood penalty*: The book *Selling Women Short* highlights that men who have children are paid more than their single counterparts (men are perceived to be more motivated when they are providers), but when women have children, they receive less compensation than their single counterparts (women are perceived to be less dedicated when they are mothers). Given that our jobs involve a lot of risk-return calculations, it might be particularly difficult for women in IM to stomach this "motherhood penalty." As one of our interviewees put it, "Women in our industry who go part-time after having kids, and end up with correspondingly part-time economics, might calculate the NPV [net present value] of the career under these circumstances and decide it's not worth it."

2. *Delayed promotion penalty*: This issue is (obviously) part of our "equalize promotion" challenge, but we reference it here in the "equalize pay" section as well, because it is a direct contributor to the wage gap. The impact of the promotion delay is that by year twenty of her career, a woman promoted every three years compared with a male promoted every two years earns 75 cents to his dollar. At the end of a forty-year career, this means 33 percent lower total compensation for women compared with men.

3. *Taking time off*: Often women take a midcareer pause to care for young children without understanding the cost of this decision. Goldman Sachs calculates a 20 percent hit to lifetime earnings for a woman taking a five-year career hiatus to look after her kids.[18]

Echoing the earlier quote, we also wonder whether females in IM use their analytical capabilities to calculate the NPV of their lifetime earnings and choose to opt out because the opportunity cost of exiting is lower for them than for their male counterparts as a result of the combination of the motherhood penalty, delayed promotion to PM, and lower subjective bonuses. Another angle on this is the economic penalty for part-time/flexible work arrangements, which some of the most progressive firms in our industry have embraced to retain women.

Compensation in general in IM is highly sensitive and murky. (Remember back to the discussion of incentive compensation in chapter 2.) And that is precisely the problem: in an industry with low pay transparency to start with, it's not surprising that women check out because of a well-founded hunch that they'll never be compensated the same as their male peers. We believe pay transparency could improve gender diversity in IM—and we're not alone. As one of our interviewees (an investment analyst who opted out to start her own firm) told us,

> If I could change one thing about active IM, it would be greater transparency around pay. We've done a lot of obvious things in the industry to improve diversity, but it's not working. Pay transparency would help get the industry to a truly meritocratic structure, with performance rewarded appropriately versus intangible factors like "cultural fit."

Eliminating the pay discrepancy would send a clear message to women that their hard work and efforts are valued equally.

IM firms should provide pay transparency—even at an aggregated level—to show that there is no difference in what they pay men and women. It goes without saying, we hope, that if there *is* a gender pay gap, firms should take steps to correct it. Because we are by nature focused on return on investment, increasing our understanding and perception of our potential lifetime earnings in IM will help retention. Before you throw shade on the idea, we'll give you a real-life example.

In January 2019, Citigroup became the first U.S. bank to publish its global median pay gap. The headline number: women's pay globally was 71 percent of the median male pay.[19] Citi believes that increasing transparency will allow its stakeholders—managers, board members, shareholders, and employees—to hold it accountable for narrowing this gap. The bank also made senior-level executives accountable for increasing diversity within the management ranks at the company, with a commitment to increasing to at least 40 percent the number of female assistant vice presidents through managing directors. A year later, in its most recent update on the pay gap, Citi reported a reduction of 200 bps (to 27 percent).[20]

Similarly, in the 1990s, some Canadian universities were required to provide pay transparency for higher-earning individuals. A study of the effect of this reporting found a 30 percent reduction in the male-female salary gap.[21] Shouldn't all companies use data analytics to identify and eliminate pay gaps? To put this into our own industry's terminology, the return on this investment will accrue to shareholders in the long run.

Our charge to IM firms is, once again, use technology to your advantage. Mine your own data and ensure that pay inequity does not exist at your firm.

Equalize the Culture

When it comes to promotion and pay, data-driven approaches can reap substantial rewards. But our final directive is less tangible than promotion and pay initiatives—yet the most important of our equality challenges. To improve gender diversity, cultures must change. What follows are a set of recommendations that we believe can help IM's male-dominated culture evolve into a more welcoming one for both women and minorities.

This Is Not Just Women's Work—Creating "Advocates" and "Allies"

"Women and people of color cannot carry the burden alone," says White Men as Full Diversity Partners (WMFDP). With a name selected for its shock value, WMFDP's leadership development model helps managers understand the impact they can have as senior leaders and role models to bring about transformative change in their organization. Men Advocating Real Change (MARC), a catalyst initiative, is a research-based program for men focused on empowering them to promote and help achieve workplace diversity.

Although the majority of our white male peers would like to work with more women and people of color, research shows that there are three barriers to all-out advocacy even among "woke" men: fear, apathy, and lack of awareness.[22]

Men's fear is largely driven by their concern that they could lose status and privilege. They also fear the reaction of their male colleagues and wonder whether actively supporting gender equality undermines their masculinity. Unfortunately, the #metoo era has instilled another fear in our male peers: some are afraid of doing something wrong— that their mentoring intentions could be misconstrued. A sample Bloomberg headline: "Wall Street Rule for the #Metoo Era: Avoid Women at All Cost."[23]

As for apathy, it's easy to understand why men simply might not care. What is the incentive for men to be active supporters of gender equality in their organizations when plum PM roles are scarce enough even for the males in the organization?

Yet we feel that the last barrier is the most problematic: lack of awareness of the problem. We have shared our hypothesis that the biggest challenge for women in IM is not the men who blatantly discriminate against them but, rather, the much larger group of male managers who claim they "don't see color or gender, only numbers" in their teams. Add to this a lack of awareness about the benefits of diversity, and you end up with the industry as it stands today: populated by men—some oblivious, some well-meaning—who don't see a need for change.

Highlighting the existence and impact of gender bias is essential for eliminating apathy and increasing awareness among our male colleagues. And in turn, vocal support for existing female PMs and active efforts to increase their numbers from senior men can help to allay the fears of male colleagues.

Men who have a keen sense of fair play and are aware of the gender imbalance in the industry are more likely to be identified by colleagues as "gender equity champions."[24] As organizations adapt to changes in the global workforce generally, gender equity champions will be, in our opinion, likely to rise further in their careers than their gender-ignorant counterparts.

Advocates and allies have different roles in promoting gender diversity. An advocate has a strong, measurable track record of supporting women. Advocates are vocal proponents of gender diversity both within and outside their organization. Through industry networks, professional societies, and other forums, they are on record promoting the benefits of increasing the number of women in the industry.

In contrast, allies have self-identified as being willing to support gender diversity, but they might not be publicly vocal in their commitment. Nonetheless, they are just as important for the advancement of women as advocates. Advocates are visible and have the time, energy, and even charisma to, well, advocate for diversity. Clearly, people with this unique combination of skill and bandwidth are in the minority. We should not overlook the larger, mostly silent majority of allies who would act if they only knew what to do—and if that to-do list were easy to integrate into their busy careers.

Research has shown the key elements of effective allyship. In IM, where white males are the dominant and privileged group—that is, PMs—allies need to come from this cohort. They must be institutionally supported with the right kind of bias training that emphasizes their agency rather than indicting them and that provides clear, quantifiable metrics about the positive impact of diversity. Finally, they need opportunities to transmit their newly acquired knowledge within the firm and outside it and to hone their ally skills via mentoring and advocacy of women.[25]

Diversity Programs and Bias Training as Agents of Cultural Change

Is diversity and bias training the best place to recruit allies? Many companies duly send their employees to classes on reducing unconscious bias. Unfortunately, research indicates that these classes sometimes backfire and lead to *increased* bias, particularly when the training is perceived to be threatening to the dominant group—and when that dominant group is white men.[26] Iris Bohnet, one of the foremost experts on bias in the workplace, found that increased bias subsequent to training designed to counteract it results from "moral licensing."[27] In other words, people who go through bias training give themselves license to engage in less moral or more biased behavior as a result.

We will put on our mom hats here for a minute to understand, and even sympathize with, this backlash—and propose a solution. In the same way that children respond better to parenting that encourages positive behaviors rather than reprimands negative ones, we believe reframing unconscious bias training as "ally training" could be part of the solution. There is some support for the success of this type of reframing: at one university, for example, 91 percent of male faculty attending ally training emerged with the belief that they could help create a more equitable climate for women faculty in their department.[28] Rather than point out the deficiencies of our male colleagues, let's encourage and empower them to become allies.

Although 90 percent of companies have diversity programs, a Boston Consulting Group study found that only a quarter of women felt like those programs benefited them.[29] Obviously, all diversity programs are not created equal—but which ones actually work? A *Harvard Business Review* study found that the most successful diversity initiatives share three principles: engaging managers to help solve the problem via counseling and training, exposing managers to people from diverse backgrounds, and holding managers accountable for change.[30]

Counseling and Training for Managers in IM

Counseling can help managers avoid many of the traps that disadvantage women as they progress through their careers. Research has found that the best assignments are given disproportionately to men. (Recall our low-value seats discussion in chapter 6.) Additionally, "office housework," like housework at home, is often disproportionately assigned to women. Echoing data from the home front,[31] the OECD[32] found that women work more hours than men—but more of those hours were in unpaid rather than paid work. This is a problem with an easy solution: ensure that the distribution of "housekeeping" tasks reflects the gender makeup of your workforce.

Mentor and Sponsor Women—Informally, Organically, and Formally

You heard a lot of women talk about mentors and sponsors in chapter 6—mentors being people who talk about you when you're in the room and sponsors being those who advocate for you when you aren't there. Women need both, and for the foreseeable future these are going to skew male.

Your coauthors have benefited from both formal and informal mentoring and sponsorship throughout their careers, and we have paid it forward by advocating for young women. One of us had the dubious, but effective, habit of drinking a tad too much at off-site meetings before cornering a hapless [male] senior manager to launch into a passionate pitch for one of her analyst protégées to be made a PM. Sponsorship doesn't have to happen in low-lit rooms with alcohol; it's appropriate and vital to convey information to senior managers during 360-degree performance reviews, and to lobby for female performers to get plum roles. Some IM firms have exhaustive review processes that incorporate feedback from everyone on the investing team, and women should use that opportunity to sing the praises of their female coworkers ahead of, on par with, and behind them in the pipeline. Before you accuse us of sexism, we will remind you that men do this all the time.

Most of what needs to happen for women is informal and organic advocacy, because that is how corporate culture works. But formal mentoring programs have a role to play as well—and mentorship can be a two-way street. A *Harvard Business Review* article, "Why Diversity Programs Fail and What Works Better," reports that mentoring helps chip away at biases by creating cognitive dissonance. When managers are exposed to talented individuals who don't resemble them and are tasked with advocating for them in promotion decisions and helping them get the training the employees need to move into new roles, they learn to undo their biases. When someone mentors and sponsors a person outside his demographic, he often discovers her to be as deserving as her majority counterparts.[33]

Provide Networking Opportunities

The word "networking" fills some of us with dread. But as you might recall from chapter 6, many of our interviewees believe that women (including themselves, in some cases) chronically underinvest in networking. It can be really awkward to lurk outside the office of a super-introverted senior male PM to run some ideas by him (trust us, we have been there, and it's cringy). But to date, these types of frequently random interactions have been foundational to career momentum in IM.

What follows is the description of a small group of like-minded investors that was cofounded by one of your authors, which we believe provides a good template for IM firms looking to formalize, routinize, and—above all—*equalize* networking opportunities. Although the Iron Skirts targets rising female executives outside the IM industry, its lessons are relevant inside it as well.

The Iron Skirts is a small group of women with extensive experience investing in public and private companies. The group was originally formed to provide support and networking opportunities for its members. Over time we broadened our discussions to include female executives in finance and industry—the women who picked up the phone when we called with a question about earnings or strategy for one of the companies we follow.

We have spent much of our careers focused on companies in the industrials and materials sectors and related subsectors, including chemicals, aerospace and defense, oil and gas, and building products. These sectors generally have among the lowest representation of women in senior leadership, the C-suite, and the boardroom. Because the Iron Skirts believe that women, and diversity in general, add tremendous value to organizations, we set out to help improve gender balance in the companies we are tasked with researching and investing in. Iron Skirts members educate rising female executives in traditionally male-dominated fields about Wall Street. We are seeking to give women a leg up in the promotion process, as they can be passed over for top jobs because they lack the necessary financial acumen and understanding of Wall Street that rising to the top of the company requires.

We believe a similar network for aspiring analysts and PMs would create networking opportunities for the women who have a hard time creating them on their own. Using the Iron Skirts example, our roadmap is simple.

Listen and learn: The Iron Skirts hosts informal dinners with senior male and female executives from industry. The discussions run broader than women's issues. The intention is to learn more about what is happening in industry to help identify the leading cultures and best practices. Within IM firms, a formal network of analysts and PMs, both male and female, who enjoy casual dinners with meaningful discussions about investments and firm initiatives can give women a literal seat at the table—and can diminish the shadowy informal dinners, golf outings, and less wholesome get-togethers that are typically the domain of men. (There are only so many nights in a month when you get a "hall pass" from the wife, right? Make sure you use them equitably.)

Educate: We have often found that up-and-coming female executives are extremely competent in their areas of expertise but have limited exposure to investors, and they lack an understanding of what investors want to hear and how they want to hear it. Based on our own experiences and expectations, we prepare women to make more successful investor presentations. This has an analog in the analyst ranks: female investment analysts tend to know their industries and companies inside out but lack the lingo and awareness to make a case for their promotion to PM.

Promote: The Iron Skirts works to promote women's advancement both in organizations and into board positions. Again, the analog is obvious: advocacy and sponsorship within the IM firm for women.

Connect: The Iron Skirts connects rising female executives in different firms and industries to enable them to share ideas and experiences directly with other leaders outside their own organization. This is an extension of the small support group for our own industry that was the foundation of the Iron Skirts. Although it's vital to have networking opportunities within our firms, we also need to build support networks outside them—to share best practices, vet ideas, compare compensation notes, and (should it come to that) line up our next job.

Purge "Bro Culture" Artifacts—and Consider Replacing Some Golf Outings with SoulCycle Classes

As discussed, we don't view our industry as a particularly bad actor in the #metoo era. But the sheer number of men who populate it can lead to the frat house mentality personified in Hollywood movies. Happily, the drugs and strippers are no more (at least, in the office), but the sports talk, excessive drinking, cigar smoking, and poker games still feature in many off-site gatherings and business trips. This is more than just exchanging golf clubs for spinning bikes; it's about rethinking our socializing traditions. Although we are not telling our bosses to prohibit happy hours—we enjoy a good one ourselves—we think that there are more productive and inclusive ways to foster teamwork and collaboration.

Conclusion: There Are Lots of Good Tools. Just Use Them.

We hope that this chapter has convinced you that there are concrete steps to take to improve gender diversity—in IM and in general. When it comes to promotion and pay, IM can rely on the toolkits provided by a wide range of third parties and on best practices across various industries.

We'll say it again. Our cultural equality charge is the most difficult one on our list—and that's because the majority of the change has to come from the majority of the workforce: our white male peers. We applaud programs aimed at making men part of the solution, and we have attempted to distill their messages into some simple advice to our male coworkers:

> Be role models by promoting diversity through your actions and words. Speak up if you hear a male colleague interrupt one of us or take credit for our ideas.

Offer to mentor and sponsor us.

Take us to lunch.

Listen carefully to our pitches and resist the siren songs of our male peers who talk louder and with more conviction than we do.

Be fair and thoughtful in your annual reviews of us; keep lists of our recommendations and remind yourself of our good calls as needed.

Run attribution at the industry level on your portfolio to see how each analyst's picks performed; don't ignore those of us covering "Brussels sprouts" industries.

Become our social justice partners, because we will all benefit from better results—and, ultimately, higher paychecks—when our portfolio management teams are better balanced.

In our final solutions chapter, we will turn our gaze outside IM to the clients who utilize it—a group we refer to as allocators. Of course, gender balance targets are most effective when they come from the top. But when they come from your clients, it can be particularly impactful—and motivating. A growing number of our institutional clients—some of the same people who are responsible for your retirement money—are agitating for more diversity among the managers of your money. But their efforts are sometimes stymied by the same structural aspects of the industry that keep women from moving up in its ranks.

12

Solutions—The Role of Allocators

I was chief investment officer for the New York City pension funds back in 2014. We were managing $160 billion, and every manager in the world who wanted to manage New York City's pension money would come to meet with me. That was great since I love investing, but I was shocked by how every time I got to anyone's organizational chart in their presentations, I'd look down at it and see that there were few if any women on their investment teams.

—SEEMA HINGORANI, FOUNDER AND CHAIR OF GIRLS WHO INVEST

One of the reasons this book is relevant to everyone, not just people in IM or considering it as a career, is that as PMs we are investing *your* money—either your 401k or retirement savings, your personal savings, or your 529 or education savings. But a substantial portion of the world's wealth is invested through savers in the financial ecosystem like the one Hingorani, quoted above, used to work for: pension plans, endowments, sovereign wealth funds, and wealthy family offices. If you're fortunate enough to have a pension, it is overseen by one of these entities. These entities allocate (hence the term "allocators") capital to separately managed accounts, various fund structures, private equity investments, and alternatives, and even make direct investments in companies, real estate, timber, commodities, and other real assets with the goal of diversifying their portfolios and enhancing returns.

In the same way that PMs are stewards of their clients' capital, allocators are fiduciaries who are responsible for the investments of millions of individuals. This chapter focuses on the roles that allocators, or the "big savers" (as opposed to individuals like us, who are "little savers") can play in helping to seed and support a more gender-balanced IM industry. Just as we gave work–life balance its own chapter, we believe that the role of the allocators is important enough to merit a separate chapter. Responsibility for increasing IM diversity is rightly placed on the shoulders of the IM firms themselves, but allocators can do their part as well. To put it in simple terms, the customer is always right—and allocators can leverage their customer status to make demands of the IM firms who serve them.

A Different—But Equally Important—Part of the Investing Supply Chain

Before we discuss how allocators are part of the solution to IM's diversity problem, we'll give you a brief description of this part of the investing supply chain. Thus far we've spent most of our time talking about mutual fund companies, because they are the biggest and best-known IM firms—the Vanguards and Fidelities of the world—and because both of us have worked for them. But there is another category of IM firms that you've probably never heard of if you're outside the industry that manages separate accounts for institutions. This part of the IM supply chain is called "institutional," as opposed to "retail" (which refers to mutual funds), and the clients it serves are, well, institutions, which run the gamut from huge state employee pension funds to tiny college endowments. One of us now works for a firm that manages 100 percent institutional money, and the other works for a firm with 50 percent institutional client funds and 50 percent retail client funds. The reason these institutions can be change agents, in the way that you can't as an anonymous investor in a mutual fund, is that they manage trillions of dollars. Money talks.

These institutional clients don't make investment decisions alone; they typically employ consultants, who advise them on how they should allocate their assets (that is, what percentage in stocks, bonds, alternatives, etc.) and which IM firms they should use to manage each asset class. Many investment banks, including Morgan Stanley, Goldman Sachs, and Bank of America, have consulting arms, and there are also lots of independent consultants, such as Wilshire. Consultants perform rigorous analysis of the managers they recommend to their institutional clients; their job looks somewhat like the job of an investment analyst who researches companies. This analysis includes, among other things, thirty-plus-page requests for proposals (RFPs), on-site due diligence visits, quarterly updates, and intensive portfolio metrics and returns analysis. Having been through this due diligence process multiple times, the author who is more involved in this part of IM can tell you that it is somewhat like a gynecological exam, except more personal.

Case Study: Superstar Female Investor Who Couldn't Find Any Clients

We gave you a brief introduction to hedge funds in chapter 1. Hedge funds often start the way tech firms do: with a couple of guys in a garage. In theory, the barriers to entry are low and thus more friendly to women—but hedge funds are one of the least diverse sectors of IM. The ability to raise hedge fund capital is linked to professional networks, which generally translates into some version of "old boy" networks. You might be thinking that women aren't as good at hedge fund management as men, because this type of investing requires a more aggressive personality type. If so, think again. Aggarwal and

Boyson (2016)[1] studied the returns of male versus female hedge fund managers and found that, when controlling for survivor bias, women significantly outperformed men. The fact that women are underrepresented in this field yet still manage to deliver superior returns suggests that allocators of capital have a higher standard for women hedge fund founders than they do for those founded by men.

Take Samantha Greenberg. Described as a hedge fund rising star, in January 2016, she launched Margate Capital in a year that was described as "dismal" for hedge fund start-ups.[2] As a former partner at Paulson & Co. (yes, *that* Paulson—of *The Big Short* fame) with stints in Goldman Sachs's Special Situations Group and at Chilton, a well-respected hedge fund, Samantha had a dream résumé. Unfortunately, her résumé didn't translate into success. She launched with a $130 million seed investor, but when she closed shop in 2019, it was only $215 million. During those three years the S&P was up 32 percent—which implies (we don't have access to her return and fund flow data) that she raised a measly $50 million on top of that initial seed capital.

Why couldn't Samantha translate her superior résumé and skill set into a multibillion-dollar hedge fund? In the pages that follow, we'll show you why it's not that easy for two girls in a garage to find seed capital.

Some Allocators Are Talking the Talk

We are happy to report that there are a lot of headlines about large institutions seeking diverse managers for their portfolios. It might surprise you to find out that this progressive charge is being led by government entities (which are not typically viewed as the most dynamic participants in any arena). New York State has allocated $21 billion (roughly 10 percent of its assets) to MWBE managers.[3] What are MWBEs? They are minority-and women-owned business enterprises, firms that are majority-owned by minority or women entrepreneurs.

(Note that it has to be one or the other—a firm doesn't qualify with, say, 25 percent women and 25 percent minority ownership.) New York City also has an emerging managers initiative (focused on IM firms that manage less than $2 billion) and a commitment to MWBE IM firms. It has told its consultants that they will be put on notice if they don't include MWBE recommendations. CalPERS, the pension fund for California state government workers, instituted an emerging manager program with meaningful, measurable goals. (We'll give you a depressing footnote on the last of these right here on the page: CalPERS announced at the end of 2019 that it was slashing most of its allocation to these managers, along with traditional managers, due to underperformance and fee structures.[4] Unfortunately, the MWBE push is colliding with the passive share shift, and in some cases the latter is winning.)

Despite these encouraging developments, some of the anecdotes we heard during our research reminded us that we could be in for a "rinse-and-repeat" cycle. One of the successful retired PMs we spoke with talked about getting her start because some allocators were pushing for women PMs—*back in the 1980s.* Yet women's representation in IM has barely budged since this supposed big push thirty-plus years ago.

In the 1980s, the call for more female PMs came from a particular type of capital allocator: federal, state, and local pension funds and other so-called public plans that were subject to greater regulation. Although those '80s-era allocators were acting in response to a combination of the Equal Rights Amendment and Title IX considerations, today's millennial push for gender diversity is driven by a sense of equity and fairness. We are cautiously optimistic this time, because the current effort is more organic; it's coming from beneficiaries (that is, the millennials and Gen-Zers who stand to inherit their parents' wealth) who embrace ESG (environmental, social, and governance) principles. The kids are not just all right—they are more progressive than their old-school parents, who don't think to ask why the pictures in the mutual fund brochure are always of white men. One of us can testify to this personally, after her eight-year-old son asked, "Why are you the only woman, Mama?" on seeing a picture of Mama on an investor panel. The themes are broadly similar—but because the true end clients (that is, all of us little savers) are the change agents this time, we think the odds of success are better.

When large institutions with, collectively, trillions of dollars to invest start talking about their diversity targets, you can bet that they'll find firms eager to help them meet their needs. A cottage industry that describes itself as "emerging manager consultants" and "managers of emerging managers" has emerged to help institutional clients achieve their diversity targets.

By now you're probably wondering what "emerging" means. So are some of us who might qualify for that descriptor. Generally, it is defined as a firm with less than $2 billion in assets under management (AUM), although sometimes there is a distinction between equity and fixed-income managers when it comes to size. Fixed-income pools are generally larger than equity ones, and the fees are lower, so some institutions define "emerging" as less than $10 billion in AUM for fixed income.

And here is problem #1 for the emerging manager push: the chicken and egg dilemma. Small firms lack the scale and resources of large firms to invest in the systems and technology to provide the excruciating detail that consultants require in their due diligence process. We'll do some simple math here. Let's say an IM firm in growth mode manages $1 billion in a combination of investment-grade and high-yield-rated debt, with an average fee of 25 basis points for the entire portfolio (ranging from 15 to 50 bps, which is typical for fixed-income mandates). That's $2.5 million in revenue—not too shabby. But the various pricing, index, analytic, trading, and accounting systems it takes to generate the types of reports required by consultants can run $1 million annually for a firm with around ten employees. (By the way, that's a minimum number—it's hard to make it past the first round of research if you can't show you've got enough people to do the various jobs: investment research, trading, portfolio management, compliance, back office, and, of course, the marketing person who raises the money.) Labor is by far the largest cost for an IM firm; when you're already spending 40 percent of revenue on systems costs, that eats into what you can pay to attract talented employees and, of course, what you can pay your shareholders—that is, the founders of the firm.

You might have noticed that there is nothing about diversity (either gender or minority) in the description of "emerging manager," and that's by design—because the pension funds and consultants also have separate, but often overlapping, MWBE initiatives, the idea being that the small firms are more likely to be MWBE. So, IM firms like the one that employs one of us, which is majority-women-owned but has about $4 billion in fixed-income AUM, might qualify for MWBE searches at one pension plan and for both MWBE and emerging manager searches at another.

Confused yet? We're just getting started.

Here's the next problem: the definition of "women-owned firm" varies widely, and in some cases the criteria are difficult to fulfill. Verification processes vary widely for MWBE firms, which differ by state.[5] Some MWBE certifications require a personal net worth (PNW) statement from every female shareholder of the firm. Under the Metro Nashville government's certification standards, for example, this figure cannot exceed $1.38 million for any of them. The PNW ceiling is another chicken-and-egg problem, similar to the firm size issue we referenced earlier. If a woman decides to launch her own IM strategy, she is more likely to do so from the financial security of a prior job at a well-paying IM firm—which means she probably exceeds that PNW cap.

Before you suggest that bright, relatively poor young women are starting investment strategies straight out of Columbia Business School thanks to the great education they received in the Value Investing Program, we need to tell you about yet another barrier to firm founders: the performance track record. No firm will fund a first-time PM, and rightly so; it would be irresponsible to allocate capital to someone with no experience managing it. We talked about the importance of a PM's track record in chapter 2; it's the only résumé some of us will ever use. But all track records are not created equal. If you managed a mutual fund as part of a team, you don't necessarily have a portable track record, and compliance rules and regulations prevent showing unverified results in marketing presentations. Who verifies these results? The CFA Institute's GIPS (Global Investment Performance Standards) division does. Of course, this costs money (around $25,000/year)—and involves, again, a tremendous amount of paperwork and systems that can accommodate the data requests associated with GIPS compliance. The 2020 manual for GIPS compliance is 146 pages long.[6] You pretty much have to have a full-time compliance officer to comply with GIPS. Among other restrictions on how you can report your numbers, GIPS does not allow track records to be "ported" from one firm to another, the idea being that a performance record belongs to a firm, not an individual PM.

This barrier to IM firm founders is not gendered; men and women face the challenge of portable track records equally. However, this leads us to our final point about barriers, which is not unique to IM: women struggle to raise capital, so these barriers are harder for them to overcome. The Knight Bella study we referenced in the opening paragraphs of this book,[7] which found that only about 1 percent of investable assets is managed by MWBE firms, used the implicit association test (IAT) to identify bias.[8] The test measured how an allocator of assets matched words that were typically grouped together based on gender bias (e.g., "men" and "finance") compared with those that typically were not (e.g., "women" and "finance"). The IAT results indicated that implicit bias was the biggest contributor to the difference in inflows between funds managed by men versus those managed by women. When you introduce discretion into any process that has an element of diversity—in this case, the choice between allocating capital to male versus female investment managers—bias can enter into the decision-making process. The presence of unconscious bias in many different settings has been well documented, but given the focus on track records and other, objective, data in capital allocation, we were surprised that it had crept into the allocation process. On the other hand, it echoes one of the themes from earlier chapters about how the concept of IM as a meritocracy doesn't match its gender imbalance. The decision of allocators to hire a male over a female manager might include selective enforcement of required resources, reporting, and track records: for instance, "She doesn't even have a compliance officer"; "She might have had a good record at her old firm, but since it's not GIPS-compliant, we can't use it." Substitute the word "he" for "she" and see if it sounds different. We imagine it does, particularly if, thanks to male-dominated networks, the allocator has a chummy relationship with the "he."

Barriers for Allocators—We Are Sympathetic to Their Challenges

Allocators want to look "woke" in the twenty-first century sense; that is, alert to injustice and possible bias based on gender, ethnicity, etc. In 2011, a Barclays study found that there was a growing appetite among allocators and investors for women- and minority-owned hedge funds.[9] And certain categories of allocators—in particular, public funds—are making progress in this arena; as shown on the table below, a W. K. Kellogg study found that public funds were two to three times "over-allocated" to MWBE funds relative to other allocators.[10] However, before we give those public funds a pat on the back, we'll remind you of the headline statistic: only 1 percent of money is managed by women-owned firms. So if the *average* allocator is allocating 1 percent to women-owned firms, even the optically high 22.5 percent of women-owned funds represented by the public funds is, mathematically, a tiny dollar amount relative to their overall AUM.

Why is progress so hard, given the eagerness of allocators to improve diversity among their investment managers? Allocators have a fiduciary responsibility to the underlying owners of the assets they're stewarding, whether it's pensioners or charitable organizations. "Fiduciary duty" is a commonly used term in IM; it endows the fiduciary in question with the responsibility to manage the assets with the best interests of the beneficiaries in mind and without conflict of interest or self-interested actions. Under the "prudent person [or investor] rule" (happily, changed from "prudent man" in its initial conception), a fiduciary is held to the standards of common sense and basic risk management when overseeing pools of money.

The Employment Retirement Income Security Act (ERISA) includes similar directives and standards for the people tasked with oversight of retirement assets. ERISA includes sensible rules, such as limits on how much a corporation's pension plan can invest in its own stock (so that employees of companies that go bankrupt don't see their pensions evaporate at the same time as their paychecks), and it imposes other requirements that are intended to codify the fiduciary responsibilities for managing the retirement savings for the fund's beneficiaries. These requirements have been cited as one reason that pension plans cannot use criteria other than "best performance" to allocate capital to diverse IM firms.

These legal and ethical standards, which are reasonable, can tie allocators' hands when it comes to funding MWBE IM firms. When W. K. Kellogg began using diversity criteria to hire investment managers, some of the foundation's trustees expressed concerns over whether they were meeting their fiduciary obligations when hiring diverse managers.[11] In particular, two questions arose: Did these managers represent the "best talent available" (a typical evaluation standard in IM)? And was there concentration risk given the small size of these firms?

Some board members also believe that small firms are inherently more risky and that it is safer to go with tried-and-true name brand firms. The one of us at a small, majority-women owned IM firm runs up against the small-firm risk bias all the time. We counter this with a couple of data-driven approaches: we run numbers to show that our results are superior to those of the competitor currently being used by the prospect, and we show that size can actually be a barrier to outperformance in asset classes like high-yield debt because of trading and liquidity challenges. And the prospect nods, smiles, and sends us on our way without an allocation.

The Best Talent Available

We discussed the small number of studies comparing female and male returns in chapter 2. Although those studies showed mixed results, the performance of women is at least as good as that of men, so we find the best talent argument to be flawed from a data perspective. And the elephant in the room, which we've referenced throughout the book, is the failure of active investment managers to beat their benchmarks—so if anything, the best talent argument should drive allocators toward passively managed funds.

Additionally, we shared with you several unpopular (or even, "unsexy") backwaters of the IM landscape—emerging markets, ESG, and others— where women have found it easier to become PMs because their male counterparts weren't interested. These areas have proven higher alpha (i.e., active management has outperformed benchmarks) and provide some interesting women-owned firm opportunities for allocators.

Small-Firm Risk

Perhaps we sounded unsympathetic with our earlier comments about small-firm risk. We recognize that allocators face a couple of legitimate issues with small IM firms. The first is concentration risk. Let's say you're New York State, with $200 billion in AUM across four to five large asset classes (equities, fixed income, alternatives, etc.). If you decide to fund an emerging manager, your allocation might dwarf the other portfolios that are managed by the firm. This is a common structural barrier to small IM firms; clients like company when they invest, and they don't like to be more than 50 percent of a manager's assets.

Second, as discussed earlier, smaller firms lack the financial resources to invest in all the systems, not to mention people, that fill in all the blanks on the RFPs. Of course, this is circular: less capital is allocated to women-run funds, which means that their AUM is smaller, hence they have fewer fees to fund the build-out of their business, thereby keeping their AUM smaller, meaning that they continue to be too small to attract more investment dollars.

In the words of the industry body National Association of Investment Companies (NAIC),

> The overall percentage of women and minority owned investment companies remains woefully low as well. The net result is a proverbial chicken and egg problem for investors and would-be investment managers alike. Without a larger universe of existing diverse asset managers, it seems unlikely that AUM will grow rapidly. After all, many institutional investors (public and corporate pensions, endowments, foundations, insurance companies, etc.) have limitations on their General Partner ("GP") concentration, or the amount of a money manager's total and fund assets they control. And without the ability to raise assets, it seems unlikely that the number of diverse investment management firms will grow exponentially, which may leave investors without the option of diversifying across a sufficient pool of diverse managers.[12]

Hear, hear.

Solutions for Allocators

How do allocators, many of whom have legal and regulatory fiduciary duty, overcome these hurdles? We'll give you a couple of real-life case studies.[13] Verizon's Investment Management Corp., like other pension plans, is governed by ERISA, as well as complex U.S. Department of Labor laws. But rather than take the "ERISA says we can't" approach, in 2010, Verizon dug a little deeper and found that the law allowed its pension to include social criteria in investment manager selection as long as those providers were otherwise qualified based on standard ERISA compliance criteria. This gave Verizon

Investment Management Corp. the latitude to seek out minority- and women-owned investment managers. These managers also met the plan's other selection criteria: "high-performance track record, stable portfolio management teams, understandable investment process, high peer group rankings and an established asset allocation."[14] In the same vein, Princeton's endowment chief has publicly advocated for more diversity in the institution's investment managers.[15]

Allocators like Verizon and Princeton should spend time convincing other trustees who are not yet diversity advocates of the merits of their approach. These fiduciaries need to overcome traditional biases about smaller managers and instead look at how adding diverse managers is an opportunity to find new sources of alpha and to diversify away from underperforming managers.

We also think the government could increase its efforts, using Title IX as a blueprint. Title IX promoted equality for female athletes in federally funded educational institutions, and it worked; the number of women participating in high school sports has increased by 1,057 percent and the number of women participating in college sports by 614 percent thanks to Title IX.[16] Knowing how well the government's Title IX nudge of the educational institutions worked, we would applaud any such official effort—for example, at the PGBC (the federal entity responsible for overseeing corporate pensions and administering them for bankrupt corporations)—to use an approach like Title IX with respect to pensions.

Allocators Should Support Alternative Portable Track Records

As discussed, the lack of portable track records is an impediment to any PM looking to start her own fund. IM firms don't have any incentive to make it easier for their PMs to leave (particularly their few-and-far-between female PMs), so we understand not wanting to put this magical résumé into too many hands. We would thus place the onus back on the allocators and the CFA Institute's GIPS division.

Rather than enforce stringent track record requirements, allocators should look behind the curtain and be more flexible when examining the returns that a manager has generated. Don't be afraid of unaudited data. And the GIPS compliance certification process should be more accessible, particularly as it relates to the lack of results portability from one firm to another.

Sponsoring Conferences to Provide Exposure for MWBE Firms

As MWBE-oriented searches gain momentum, several conferences have sprung up to bring MWBE IM firms and allocators together. Opal Group hosts semiannual emerging manager summits, which provide (for a fee, of course) IM firms with panel and speaking opportunities and a networking venue. Other conferences are in development. We support these events and the allocators who sponsor them and applaud their objective of profiling firms and investment strategies that meet gender diversity targets—as represented by either ownership or investment management teams that are diverse (i.e., majority female PMs).

ESG Isn't Just About the Investment Strategy—It's About the People Managing It

ESG investing has become a dominant investing theme. Even passive managers, such as Blackrock, are pushing the companies they own to engage in environmentally sustainable business practices, embrace good social practices, and implement good governance in their organizations. Blackrock CEO Larry Fink has put companies on notice that they risk seeing capital withheld if they don't make progress on these fronts.

Any allocator who is looking for an IM firm to manage an ESG strategy should consider the firm's makeup as part of the ESG mandate.

It's one thing to allocate capital to Generation Investment Management (GIM), one of the best-known ESG managers. Why shouldn't allocators equally push for GIM's leadership team, which is currently 20 percent female,[17] to be more diverse? Just as we suggested in chapter 11 that IM firms engaged in ESG should turn their ESG lenses on themselves, we issue a similar call to arms for allocators. They risk hypocrisy by describing their portfolios as ESG when the people they select to manage them are not.

It's Time to Lift the Veil

Let's say you've got money invested in a pension plan and want to know how diverse your management team is. Unfortunately, it's a struggle to find out who exactly is responsible for managing your money. Lobbyist Robert Raben founded a nonprofit that pushes for diversity in money management funds. Perhaps unsurprisingly, he finds it hard to get information about the demographics of his outside advisors.[18] If you're one of millions of pensioners, chances are you won't be able to find any data about the demographics of the investment managers responsible for it.

Disclosure by allocators is voluntary and firm specific, but we encourage all of them to disclose how gender-diverse their investment managers are. When Seema Hingorani asked for the organizational charts of the IM firms she was using, she was likely one of the only people asking that question. We encourage an industry-wide initiative that promotes disclosure by allocators of the gender diversity of their outsourced investment management teams.

Change the Evaluation Process to Change the Outcome

One of the solutions we proposed in chapter 11 for promoting more women at IM firms was the joint evaluation. We have a similar recommendation for allocators: include at least one gender-diverse firm in every RFP. When women-owned firms are evaluated against other firms rather than individually, they are less likely to be discriminated against in the manager selection process.

In their study of returns of diverse private equity managers, the NAIC suggested,

> an easy step that many investors could take is to ensure that one or more diverse private equity firms are always included in manager searches and Requests for Proposals. . . . [H]aving an inclusion rule should increase the chances that highly-qualified diverse asset managers will be seen and evaluated with their peers.[19]

Small Applause Only . . . Allocators to Date Haven't Moved the Needle

The savers of this world control trillions of dollars of capital. Our research and professional experience have introduced us to various initiatives that are designed to allocate more capital to women- and minority-owned firms. Although we applaud such efforts, at the risk of driving you crazy, we remind you once again that the impact of these initiatives is still a small drop in a huge ocean of capital.

Let's Conclude with Samantha Greenberg—and the Firm That Snatched Her Up

When we left Greenberg earlier in the chapter, she had stalled out in her capital-raising efforts. She shuttered her firm after just three years to go to work for Citadel,[20] a respected hedge fund known for its objective hiring processes. Citadel doesn't believe in reference checking, in-depth interviews, and "auditions." Instead, the firm relies largely on data rather than personality test interviews to drive its hiring decisions.[21] Like NASA and the NFL, Citadel has come up with innovative approaches to hiring. Citadel is onto something: a data-driven method of using objective performance criteria rather than subjective interviews to select PMs. Citadel is privileged to have Greenberg ironically, she's likely managing money for some of the same allocators who didn't answer her call when she was on her own.

Investment manager diversity has been described as the "hardest taboo to break."[22] We're sure that lots of female IM firm owners (including the one of us in that category) agree with this. We hope that the big savers in the financial ecosystem heed our call and take the lead—by allocating more of their capital to firms that are either majority-owned by women or that invest directly in funds where the PM is female or the PM team is gender balanced. It's time for the allocators to put *your* money where their intentions lie and create a diverse portfolio of investments that are run by a diverse team of investment managers.

Conclusion

Our Money Management Manifesto

So, here we are—in flats, ready to move forward (although we admit that we haven't ditched our high heels; they are still in the closet ready to come out for our next finals presentation).

This book should have demystified the inner workings of investment management and elucidated the job of a portfolio manager and analyst. By now you should understand how the psycho-cultural barriers to women's advancement, common to many professional industries, are magnified by institutional and cultural norms specific to IM—and that these barriers to women's full participation also might be working against good investment results. And most of all, we hope that you share our optimism about the potential for some tangible, practical, actionable solutions to transform our workforce in the years to come.

We have, ambitiously, called our conclusion a Money Management Manifesto. It is a call to arms to IM's various participants—both insiders and outsiders. The burden of increasing the representation of women in our industry cannot fall on the shoulders of just one group; it is a broader social mandate that we hope you support. Although our book has focused narrowly on IM, we believe our conclusions apply to all industries in which the main "product" is people—whether it's consultancies and other types of financial companies, law firms, physician practices, or academia. These are the knowledge professions in which the assets "go home at night." We acknowledge that some of these industries have made more progress toward gender parity than ours, but knowing that women still struggle to make it into C-suites and onto corporate boards, we believe our manifesto is relevant and applicable beyond IM.

Throughout our manifesto we use the term "balance" repeatedly. We want to be clear up front about what it does—and doesn't—mean to us. First, we are not talking about a world in which 70 percent of PMs and analysts are women; we want equality and equal representation for men, too. As we have repeatedly stated throughout this book, we understand the power of diversity in decision-making—an industry with 10 percent male representation is as backward as our industry is currently. We are not advocating stringent 50-50 male-female guidelines. Throughout this book we have used 30 percent as the definition of a level of female participation that transitions women from salient minority to acknowledged voice. Given that we are both uninspiring marathoners (let's call us "five-hour people"), we'll employ a running analogy. The halfway point in a marathon is 30 percent—a good signpost to show that we are midway there. The ultimate goal is to go the full, 26.2-mile distance. Although we appreciate the good intentions of the 30 percent club and other organizations of setting a manageable goal when you start training (and, yes, a half-marathon seemed a *long* way when we both started training), it is just a goalpost along the way. By setting an intermediate goal we believe that our efforts to improve gender parity in IM will not succumb to the outcome of the very first marathoner, who collapsed after gasping, "We have won!" We will get to the half-marathon marker at a measured and sustainable pace; we have the long game in mind. The winners we care most about are those of you who have entrusted your money to us—and to be clear, we define "winning" as better investment results.

IM's flywheel is in perpetual motion. Its very design resists change, and we question whether running on this flywheel has left the industry's female participation stuck at 10 percent (or even going in the wrong direction). Our book has not advocated radical, revolutionary change; we have deliberately proposed solutions that work within the industry's existing framework. Though acknowledging the challenges our industry is facing that are seemingly unrelated to its lack of diversity, we don't want to throw a wrench into IM's flywheel; rather, we want to repair it in motion.

Throughout the book we have used the principles of portfolio management to illustrate the benefits of diversification (as we have called it, Portfolio Management 101), and our manifesto continues the metaphor. We look at the industry's problems the same way as would a PM who inherits a portfolio. You've learned about what PMs do, so put yourself in the shoes of a PM who wins a new account that transfers a portfolio invested entirely in tech stocks into your capable hands. As much as you like (some) tech exposure, you know that the portfolio needs to be rebalanced in the long run. Yet there are meaningful structural barriers to doing this in a short period: capital gains, transaction costs, the ability for the sell side to front-run you—which means that you have to balance the short-term and long-term interests of the portfolio's shareholders. We might question the compliance officer who overlooked such a concentrated portfolio, but there's no use blaming the PM who constructed it. The best approach, as any PM who takes over for another can tell you, is to make gradual, evolutionary rather than revolutionary changes while having a clear vision and time frame for achieving the balanced portfolio you have in mind—while also being flexible enough to react to exogenous market shocks (like, say, a pandemic) along the way. In our opinion, restructuring the IM industry's "portfolio" of PMs and analysts needs to take a similar approach.

What follows is our approach to rebalancing the IM workforce, with a long-term objective of gender parity and a short-term focus on minimizing friction, transaction costs, and the impact on IM's end clients.

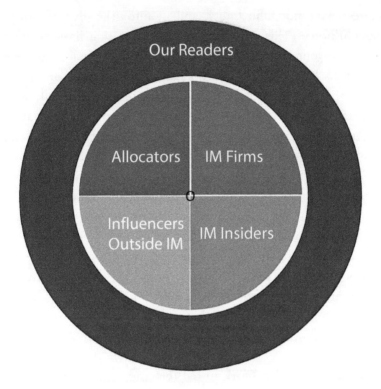

FIGURE C.1 Our money manifesto—five calls to arms.

Figure by the authors.

IM Firms: Balance Your Workforces as They Are Expected to Balance Their Portfolios

We issue a call to arms to the IM firms who employ us and to our peers—both men and women. Set gender balance goals, and hold yourselves accountable to achieving them. These goals should permeate the entire IM pipeline, from recruiting to promotion and retention, using the strategies outlined in chapters 10 and 11. Take a page out of your compliance handbooks, which include rigorous monitoring of portfolio limits, and monitor the diversification of your workforce. This means balance in recruiting investment analysts, PMs, your boards of directors, and your mutual fund boards. This means balanced pay and bonuses that are based on objective performance rather than intangible attributes that can fall sway to unconscious (and even conscious) biases. And this means balanced sponsorship and mentorship (formal and informal) of women in the organization to ensure they have a seat at the table whether or not they are physically present. Finally, we cannot emphasize it enough: IM firms *must* replace gendered cultural artifacts (the poker sessions, golf outings, random alcohol-fueled late-night conversations at off-site gatherings) with more accessible networking opportunities. And because we don't want to swing the pendulum too far in the other direction, those artifacts can't swing too far the other way: we don't want mani-pedi evenings—we want events that are open to everyone, men and women alike.

Individuals Who Work in IM (Us and Our Coworkers): Advocate for Women

We issue a call to arms to our female peers to become part of the constellation of women investors we introduced in chapter 8. These women, both those we interviewed and quoted and the many other female PMs in the industry whom we haven't mentioned by name, are there to show women—particularly junior women in the industry—that it can be done. Tell aspiring analysts and PMs how you've done it. Go to their campuses to tell them how much you love your job. Stop by their offices when a call is going against them. Take a girl to lunch (or breakfast, or coffee, or for a run, seeing as how a lot of us are runners).

Addressing the IM industry's gender imbalance can't fall onto the shoulders of women alone. We issue a call to arms to our male peers to become our allies. Show that you want things to change. When you visit campuses for recruiting events, when you're on panels, and when you're in prospect meetings, highlight both the women and the men on your team. Don't participate in "bro" events (male-only or male-dominant networking). Don't fall for the confident pitch by a male analyst while overlooking a more nuanced pitch by a female one. Just as we suggested women should do for female analysts, men should Stop by our offices when a call is going against us. Take us to lunch to show your support.

Allocators: Balance Your Capital Allocation

One of the reasons for our confidence that the gender imbalance in our industry can be addressed is that outsiders can influence where the money goes (and therefore where the investment management profits go). We issue a call to arms to capital allocators to employ the strategies in chapter 12. Adjust your evaluation criteria to cast a wider net for talented female investors. Don't lower your standards; take a hard look at them and acknowledge that some of the boxes you'd like to check do not tell you much about investment acumen. Wean yourself off reams of data to focus on results. While you're at it, boycott any fundraising conference that has the potential to objectify women. (Believe it or not, "meetings" at cabanas by the pool were still happening in 2020 before COVID-19 sent everyone to Zoom.) Look at this the same way that you boycott blood diamonds to send a message to insurgents in war zones; you'll send a message to conference organizers to lift their game.

Influencers Outside the Industry: Encourage Balanced Coverage

We haven't mentioned them explicitly before, but there are people with the ability to influence the IM gender equation. We issue a call to arms to members of the media to cover our industry with the balance it deserves. Most of IM is not *The Wolf of Wall Street*—Hollywood has done us a disservice. The majority of us take our fiduciary duties to our clients very seriously and want to achieve good results so they can send their kids to college, buy a house, and retire in time to enjoy the last decade or two of their lives. Throw some sunshine on what we do, and stop running sensationalist headlines about rogue hedge fund dudes, casting them as investing archetypes rather than the exceptions they represent. Write stories about the dull ones among us. Quote women in investing articles. Create a Rolodex with our names. (You might start with our constellation chapter.)

We issue a call to arms to universities to track gender metrics for your on-campus investment clubs, and hold them to 30 percent female membership standards with a long-term objective of parity. If you can't find the women you need, figure out why, and cast a wider net with more exposure to females in the industry and to the career in general. Recruit more female finance professors, and push your faculty to include female practitioners as guest lecturers.

Our Final Call to Arms Is to Our Readers

We end the book with our final call to arms—which is to you. Ask "Who manages my money?" You might be asking your financial advisor; you might be calling Schwab to find out where to find the prospectus for the mutual funds you hold; you might be looking around at the PMs next to you. Find people to ask and hold them accountable for getting you the answer. The lack of IM diversity doesn't just affect those of us in the industry—it impacts society more widely. As we have repeatedly stated, IM's failure to generate index-beating returns could result from the lack of diversity in our ranks. By demanding to know who manages your money, you will shine a brighter light on our problem.

Since the inception of investment management, women who participate in the industry have been dancing backwards in high heels to get ahead. We have been taking our cues from our leading dance partners—with mixed results for an industry confronting challenges from new business models (passives) and increasing costs. Our manifesto envisions an industry with gender parity, fairness, and equity for all its participants, with the ultimate goal of better results for the people whose money we manage.

Acknowledgments

Twenty years ago, two women who love to run met through a group of wonderful and inspiring women called the Running Ladies in Los Angeles. Both of us worked in investment management, and we kept in touch over the years despite living on separate coasts. Decades later, a chance encounter in Central Park, facilitated by running lady Nancy Linn, found us asking each other the same question: why aren't there more women like us? That conversation led to a two-year collaboration that resulted in this book.

We are both fortunate to work at firms that are led by female CEOs who were supportive of our efforts to write this book, Franklin Templeton Investments and Barksdale & Associates.

The list of people who helped this book come into being is extensive. We thank the numerous friends and colleagues who made introductions on our behalf, as many of our interviews would not have been possible without their referrals. These investors are quoted throughout our book, some with attribution; the thoughts and experiences of many others filtered into our themes and insights, even if they did not make it verbatim into these pages. These introductions were not exclusively to potential interviewees; we also had vital referrals to researchers studying the topic of diversity, other authors, our contacts' bosses in finance, and, in one case, someone's wife. We are also grateful to the assistants who helped us get time on busy schedules and chased their bosses down to get signatures for quote attribution forms. Many people sent us articles of interest. Some people (who were not our moms) even asked to buy advance copies of our book.

Both of us built, and continue to build, a strong network for our successful investment management careers. Similarly, writing this book required a strong extended network of people who believed in what we were doing, saw the merit in addressing the lack of diversity in the industry, and worked with us to move this project forward. You might not have been named here directly (in fact, some of you asked not to be!), but please know that without you, this book would not exist. Yes, we did lots of research, like the diligent analysts we are in our day jobs, but the soul of our book relies on the willingness of so many women and men to talk to us, both on and off the record.

Our undergraduate chapter is a collaborative effort between Rutgers University Professor Lisa Kapolowitz and her students Osayre Gomez, Ty-Lynn Johnson, Emanuel Marques, and Bernadette McCormick. The result of their tireless efforts and persistence is that this chapter reflects the views of undergraduates across the country rather than simply the Northeast.

Columbia Business School supported our efforts by allowing us to survey the student investment management club, as well as providing access to the Career Management Center. We greatly appreciate the contributions of Laurie Boockvar and Jon Hicks to chapter 5, as well as the MBA students who spoke to us, in particular our anonymous case study student, "Tina."

The computer programming used to analyze the text of the many interviews that we conducted was written by Deepti Kalikivaya.

This book benefited greatly from the early feedback that we received from friends and family, specifically, Todd Jacobson, Terry Roberts, Ellen Kettle, Carolyn Herzog, Bonnie Orlowski, Jennifer Mulroy, and Dawn Starks.

Acknowledgments

    Finally, this book would not have come into existence without the patience of our families (including a pandemic puppy), who stuck with us through multiple drafts, late-night interview transcriptions, and multiple Zoom conversations that replaced in-person meetings during our final months of editing.

APPENDIX

Organizations Mentioned in This Book

In our research for this book, we discovered many organizations that focus on improving diversity in corporate America. The information below refers specifically to those organizations mentioned in our book.

100 Women in Finance

100 Women in Finance's more than 15,000 members, including the two authors of this book, strengthen the global finance industry by empowering women to achieve their professional potential at each career stage. Its members inspire, equip, and advocate for a new generation of industry leadership in which women and men serve as investment professionals and executives who are equal in achievement and impact. Through education, peer engagement, and impact, the organization furthers the progress of women who have chosen finance as a career and enables their positive influence over young pre-career women. https://100women.org.

Girls Who Invest

Girls Who Invest (GWI) is dedicated to increasing the number of women in portfolio management and executive leadership in the asset management industry. GWI's program is composed of an intensive four-week on-campus educational program immediately followed by paid six-week internships at leading investment management firms in the United States, UK, and Canada. Its strategy is simple: investment firms say they do not see enough résumés from women, so GWI is creating a pipeline of motivated young women who are prepared to succeed on investment teams in the investment management industry and who leave the program with an ongoing and sustainable community. http://www.girlswhoinvest.org.

Phelps Forward

Phelps Forward wants to develop and deliver diverse business leaders of the future. The organization provides career counseling, networking, and job placement for first-generation college students and graduates, all women, from top-tier colleges. PF works closely with its business partners and colleges to ensure mutually successful job placements. http://www.phelpsforward.com.

Rock the Street, Wall Street

Rock the Street, Wall Street focuses on moving girls forward in the field of finance. Female financial professionals lead classroom workshops on money management and more during a five-week period. RTSWS has a cutting-edge open-source curriculum ripped from the headlines and discusses public policy, economic policy, and stock and bond markets. The organization's workshops have covered topics ranging from credit card debt to auto financing to blockchain. The program includes life skills, exposure, and community building. https://rockthestreetwallstreet.com.

Bloomberg New Voices Initiative

The New Voices Initiative program was founded and sponsored by Bloomberg to diversify newsroom sources and ensure fairness and balance in coverage. The initiative has created a database on women newsmakers in business and finance who have received media training and are ready to be interviewed as authoritative voices in finance.

Women in Investing (WIN)

Founded in 2010 by Lakshmi Bhojraj, Breazzano Family Executive Director of the Parker Center for Investment Research at Cornell University, the Women in Investing Conference is designed to educate undergraduate and MBA students about the rewarding career opportunities available to women in investment management, a field in which women are vastly underrepresented. More information can be found at https://www.johnson.cornell.edu/parker-center-for-investment -research/mba-women-in-investing-conference/ and https://www.johnson .cornell.edu/parker-center-for-investment-research/undergraduate-women -in-investing-conference/.

CFA Institute

The CFA Institute is the world's largest association of investment professionals. The organization offers the Chartered Financial Analyst designation, the Certificate in Investment Performance Management designation, and the Investment Foundations Certificate. The CFA Institute provides services to its members to help them stay current about industry developments through continuing education events, conferences, seminars, webcasts, and publications. http://www.cfainstitute.org.

Investment Company Institute (ICI)

ICI is the leading global association for regulated funds including mutual funds, ETFs, closed-end funds, and unit investment trusts. The institute encourages members to adhere to high ethical standards, promotes public financial literacy of both fund types and investing in general, and focuses on advancing the interests of investment funds and their shareholders, directors, and advisors. http://www.ici.org.

Notes

Prologue

1. Throughout this book we use the term "investment management," or IM, to refer generally to the management of other people's money. We define this in greater detail, along with some other basic terms, at the end of the prologue.
2. Josh Lerner and Bella Research Group, *Diversifying Investments: A Study of Ownership Diversity in the Asset Management Industry*, Knight Foundation, January 29, 2019, https://knightfoundation.org/reports/diversifying-investments-a-study-of-ownership-diversity-and-performance-in-the-asset-management-industry/; and Laura Pavlenko Lutton and Erin Davis, *Morningstar Research Report: Fund Managers by Gender*, Morningstar, 2015, https://www.ft.com/content/6bc474d6-b578-11e6-961e-a1acd97f622d.
3. CFA Institute, *Driving Change: Diversity and Inclusion in Investment Management*, 2018, https://www.cfainstitute.org/en/research/survey-reports/diversity-and-inclusion.

1. An Overview of the Active Investment Management Industry

1. Investment Company Institute, FAQs & Resource Centers, https://www.ici.org/faqs/faq/mfs/faqs_mf_shareholders, accessed November 4, 2020.
2. According to the SEC website (https://www.sec.gov/fast-answers/answersm-fredemptionshtm.html), a mutual fund has up to seven days to pay redemption proceeds from the date of the request. However, most mutual funds, based on our experience, pay proceeds to investors in two days.

3. Berlinda Lui and Philiip Brzenk, "SPIVA® U.S. Scorecard," *S&P Dow Jones Indices, McGraw Hill Financial, Mid Year* (2019), https://www.spglobal.com/spdji/en/documents/spiva/spiva-us-mid-year-2019.pdf.

4. "InvestingWithoutPeople" (memorandum), https://www.oaktreecapital.com/docs/default-source/memos/investing-without-people.pdf, accessed November 4, 2020.

5. A ticker is a shortcut that refers to a particular security that is listed on an exchange or is otherwise publicly traded.

6. Morgan Stanley and Oliver Wyman, *Asset Managers and Wholesale Banks: Searching for Growth in an Age of Disruption*, Morgan Stanley Research, March 14, 2019, https://www.oliverwyman.com/content/dam/oliver-wyman/v2/publications/2019/mar/Asset-Managers-Wholesale-Banks-Searching-For-Growth-2019.pdf.

7. PwC, *Asset Management 2020: A Brave New World*, 2014, https://www.pwc.com/gx/en/asset-management/publications/pdfs/pwc-asset-management-2020-a-brave-new-world-final.pdf.

8. Richard Henderson, "Passive Assets Poised to Surpass Active in the US by 2021," *Financial Times*, March 14, 2019, https://www.ft.com/content/5c6bf51a-4660-11e9-a965-23d669740bfb.

9. William F. Sharpe, "The Arithmetic of Active Management," *Financial Analysts Journal* 47, no. 1 (1991): 7–9.

10. David Blitz and Milan Vidojevic, "The Performance of Exchange-Traded Funds," SSRN, October 6, 2019, https://papers.ssrn.com/sol3/papers.cfm?abstract_id=3458275.

11. Robin Wigglseworth, "Passive Attack: The Story of a Wall Street Revolution," *Financial Times*, December 20, 2018, https://www.ft.com/content/807909e2-0322-11e9-9d01-cd4d49afbbe3.

12. Julia La Roche, "Hedge Funds—There Are Too Many of Them and Most of Them Are Lousy," Yahoo Finance, May 7, 2016, https://finance.yahoo.com/news/are-there-too-many-hedge-funds-193953003.html?guccounter=1.

13. Gillian Tett, "Millennial Heirs to Change Investment Landscape," *Financial Times*, September 20, 2018, https://www.ft.com/content/59f6562a-786d-11e8-af48-190d103e32a4.

14. Fidelity Charitable, *Impact Investing on the Rise: How Financial Advisers Are Adapting*, accessed on November 4, 2020, https://www.fidelitycharitable.org/content/dam/fc-public/docs/insights/impact-investing-how-financial-advisors-are-adapting.pdf.

15. Fidelity Charitable, *Impact Investing: At a Tipping Point?*, 2018, https://www.fidelitycharitable.org/content/dam/fc-public/docs/insights/impact-investing-at-a-tipping-point.pdf. Also cited in Fidelity Charitable, *Impact Investing on the Rise*.

2. What Is a Portfolio Manager, and Why Would Anyone Want to Become One?

1. Benjamin Graham and David Dodd, *Security Analysis: The Classic 1934 Edition* (Burlington, NC: McGraw Hill, 2003).
2. Rebecca Fender, ed., *Gender Diversity in Investment Management: New Research for Practitioners on How to Close the Gender Gap* (Charlottesville, VA: CFA Institute Research Foundation, 2016), https://www.cfainstitute .org/-/media/documents/survey/gender-diversity-report.ashx.
3. Laura Pavlenko Lutton and Erin Davis, *Morningstar Research Report: Fund Managers by Gender*, Morningstar, 2015, 1–6.
4. Olivia Seddon-Daines and Yasmine Chinwala, "Diversity in Portfolio Management," New Financial, September 2018, https://newfinancial.org/diversity -in-portfolio-management/.
5. Corporate Finance Institute, "Total Compensation and CFA Salary Guide," in *CFA Salary Guide*, https://corporatefinanceinstitute.com/resources/careers /compensation/cfa-salary-compensation/.
6. Tom Maloney and Hema Parmar, "Five Hedge Fund Heads Made More than $1 Billion Each Last Year," Bloomberg.com, February 11, 2020, https://www .bloomberg.com/news/articles/2020-02-11/five-hedge-fund-heads-earned-more -than-1-billion-each-last-year.
7. Linlin Ma, Yuehua Tang, and Juan-Pedro Gómez, "Portfolio Manager Compensation in the US Mutual Fund Industry," *Journal of Finance* 74, no. 2 (2019): 587–638.
8. Jane Fuller, "Asset Managers Must Clamp Down on Their Variable Pay at the Top," *Financial Times*, September 1, 2019, https://www.ft.com/content /4fa2f941-4b20-3d1d-bocf-eb02e993ca99.
9. Stefan Ruenzi, Alexandra Niessen-Ruenzi, and Kristina Meier, "The Impact of Role Models on Women's Self-Selection in Competitive Environments," SSRN, December 14, 2017 (rev. March 25, 2020), https://papers.ssrn.com /sol3/papers.cfm?abstract_id=3087862.
10. Bob Pisani, "Active Fund Managers Trail the S&P 500 for the Ninth Year in a Row in Triumph for Indexing," CNBC, March 15, 2019, https://www.cnbc .com/2019/03/15/active-fund-managers-trail-the-sp-500-for-the-ninth-year -in-a-row-in-triumph-for-indexing.html.

3. Representation of Women in Investment Management

1. GAO, *Financial Services Industry: Trends in Management and Representation of Minorities and Women and Diversity Practices, 2007–2015* (report), November 8, 2017, https://www.gao.gov/products/GAO-18-64.

2. Exane BNP, *More Than a Woman 2019* (report), August 9, 2019. See https:// www.janushenderson.com/en-us/advisor/article/investing-in-diversity -analysing-the-investment-risks-and-opportunities/.

3. Laura Pavlenko Lutton and Erin Davis, *Morningstar Research Report: Fund Managers by Gender*, Morningstar, 2015, 1–6.

4. Rebecca Fender, ed., *Gender Diversity in Investment Management: New Research for Practitioners on How to Close the Gender Gap* (Charlottesville, VA: CFA Institute Research Foundation, 2016), https://www.cfainstitute.org /-/media/documents/survey/gender-diversity-report.ashx.

5. Laura Pavlenko Lutton, "Fund Managers by Gender: The Global Landscape" (video), Morningstar, December 16, 2016, https://www.morningstar .com/articles/785491/fund-managers-by-gender-the-global-landscape.

6. Carmen Germaine, "Missing the Mark on Diversity, Firms Retool Internships," *Ignites*, November 12, 2018, https://www.ignites.com/c/2130303 /254763.

7. Angus Foote, "Alpha Female 2019: Female Fund Managers Stuck on 10 Percent," *Citywire*, July 29, 2019, https://citywireusa.com/professional-buyer /news/alpha-female-2019-female-fund-managers-stuck-on-10/a1254304.

8. Josh Lerner and Bella Research Group, *Diversifying Investments: A Study of Ownership Diversity in the Asset Management Industry*, Knight Foundation, January 29, 2019, https://knightfoundation.org/reports/diversifying-investments -a-study-of-ownership-diversity-and-performance-in-the-asset-management -industry/.

9. Lutton and Davis, "Fund Managers by Gender."

10. Lutton, "Fund Managers by Gender: The Global Landscape."

11. Chris Tighe, "Female Engineers Flourish but Numbers Stay Stubbornly Low," *Financial Times*, October 3, 2019, https://www.ft.com/content/18e8e7ba-e112 -11e9-b112-9624ec9edc59.

12. Nick Leiber, "The Fight for Female MBAs," Bloomberg Businessweek, June 8, 2018, https://www.bloomberg.com/news/articles/2018-06-08/the-fight-for -female-mbas.

13. Claire Cain Miller, "How Medicine Became the Stealth Family-Friendly Profession," *New York Times*, August 21, 2019, https://www.nytimes.com /2019/08/21/upshot/medicine-family-friendly-profession-women.html.

14. Marianne Bertrand, Claudia Goldin, and Lawrence F. Katz, "Dynamics of the Gender Gap for Young Professionals in the Financial and Corporate Sectors," *American Economic Journal: Applied Economics* 2, no. 3 (2010): 228–55.

15. Brad M. Barber, Anna Scherbina, and Bernd Schlusche, "Performance Isn't Everything: Personal Characteristics and Career Outcomes of Mutual Fund Managers," SSRN, September 7, 2017 (rev. May 20, 2018), https://papers .ssrn.com/sol3/papers.cfm?abstract_id=3032207.

16. Alok Kumar, "Self-Selection and the Forecasting Abilities of Female Equity Analysts," *Journal of Accounting Research* 48, no. 2 (May 2010): 393–435, https:// doi.org/10.1111/j.1475-679X.2009.00362.x.

17. Kumar, "Self-Selection and the Forecasting Abilities of Female Equity Analysts."

18. Alastair Marsh, "Women Shattered the ESG Ceiling, Now the Men Want In," Bloomberg News, January 24, 2020, https://www.bloomberg.com/news /articles/2020-01-24/women-shattered-this-glass-ceiling-now-the-men -want-in.

19. Brad M. Barber and Terrance Odean, "Boys Will Be Boys: Gender, Over-confidence, and Common Stock Investment," *Quarterly Journal of Economics* 116, no. 1 (2001): 261–92.

20. Barber and Odean, "Boys Will Be Boys."

21. Madison Sargis and Kathryn Wing, *Fund Managers by Gender: Through the Performance Lens*, Morningstar, 2018, https://www.morningstar.com/lp /fund-managers-by-gender-performance-lens.

22. Maggie Wang and Lijing Wang, *Citi US CLO Scorecard*, CitiGroup Research, January 31, 2019.

23. Lu Wang, "Women Fund Managers Beating Men in Picking Stocks, Goldman Finds," Bloomberg, August 28, 2020, https://www.bloomberg.com/news /articles/2020-08-28/women-fund-managers-beating-men-in-picking-stocks -goldman-finds.

24. Kyria Capital Management, *A Deep Dive Into the Women-Run Hedge Fund Universe*, June 2015, https://www.valuewalk.com/2015/07/a-deep-dive -into-the-women-run-hedge-funds-universe.

25. CFA Institute, *Driving Change: Diversity and Inclusion in Investment Management*, 2018, https://www.cfainstitute.org/en/research/survey-reports/diversity -and-inclusion.

26. Michaela Bär, Alexandra Niessen-Ruenzi, and Stefan Ruenzi, "The Impact of Work Group Diversity on Performance: Large Sample Evidence from the Mutual Fund Industry," SSRN, September 2007, https://papers.ssrn.com/sol3 /papers.cfm?abstract_id=1017803.

27. CFA Institute, *Driving Change*.

28. Bär et al., "The Impact of Work Group Diversity on Performance."

29. Jasmin Joecks, Kerstin Pull, and Karin Vetter, "Gender Diversity in the Boardroom and Firm Performance: What Exactly Constitutes a 'Critical Mass'?," *Journal of Business Ethics* 118, no. 1 (2013): 61–72.

30. For two recent reviews of the literature on corporate board diversity and firm performance, see Renée Adams, "Women on Boards: The Superheroes of Tomorrow?," *Leadership Quarterly* 27, no. 3 (2016): 371–86, http://dx.doi .org/10.1016/j.leaqua.2015.11.001; and Deborah Rhode and Amanda Packel, "Diversity on Corporate Boards: How Much Difference Does Difference

Make?," *Delaware Journal of Corporate Law* 39, no. 2 (2014), http://www.djcl
.org/volume-39/2014-%e2%80%a2-volume-39-%e2%80%a2-number-2-2.

31. Carol Kisney Goman, "Is Your Communication Style Dictated by Your Gender?," *Forbes*, March 31, 2016, https://www.forbes.com/sites/carolkinseygoman
/2016/03/31/is-your-communication-style-dictated-by-your-gender/?sh
=1f044487eb9d.

32. Fender, *Gender Diversity in Investment Management*.

Part II: Diagnosis of IM's Gender Imbalance

1. It's annoying that although SAHM (for "stay-at-home mom") is a recognized dictionary.com word, neither SAHD (stay-at-home dad) nor SAHH
(stay-at-home husband) is. Sigh . . . or, should we say, how SAHD. . . .

2. Ronald J. Burke and Mary C. Mattis, *Women and Minorities in Science, Technology, Engineering and Mathematics: Upping the Numbers*
(Northampton, MA: Edward Elgar).

3. Ellen Carr, "Advice from One Female Portfolio Manager to Others," *Financial Times*, January 15, 2019, https://www.ft.com/content/d149a632-14ee
-11e9-a168-d45595ado76d.

4. Katty Kay and Claire Shipman, "The Confidence Gap," *Atlantic*, May 2014:
1–18, https://www.theatlantic.com/magazine/archive/2014/05/the-confidence
-gap/359815/, referring to the original study on "honest overconfidence"
by E. Reuben, P. Rey-Biel, P. Sapienza, and L. Zingales, "The Emergence
of Male Leadership in Competitive Environments," *Journal of Economic
Behavior & Organization* 83, no. 1 (June 2012): 111–17, http://dx.doi.org
/10.1016/j.jebo.2011.06.016.

4. Why Don't Women Choose Investing Careers?
The Undergraduate Pipeline

1. National Center for Education Statistics, "Table 318.30: Bachelor's, Mas-
ter's, and Doctoral Degrees Conferred by Postsecondary Institutions, by
Sex of Student and Discipline Division: 2016–17," in *Digest of Education
Statistics*, https://nces.ed.gov/programs/digest/d18/tables/dt18_318.30.asp.

2. We define "business related" as including business, management, marketing, and related support services.

3. Ayaz Nanji, "The 10 Industries Most Distrusted by US Consumers," *Mar-
ketingProfs*, September 15, 2017, https://www.marketingprofs.com/charts
/2017/32764/the-10-industries-most-distrusted-by-us-consumers.

4. Maciej Kolackowski, "The Oil Industry Has a Trust Problem—Can It Put That Right?," World Economic Forum, April 13, 2016, https://www .weforum.org/agenda/2016/04/the-oil-industry-has-a-trust-problem-can -the-industry-put-that-right/.

5. Jamie Dimon, "Unless We Change Capitalism, We Might Lose It Forever," *Time*, Davos 2020, https://time.com/collection/davos-2020/5764098/jamie -dimon-capitalism/.

6. See Rock the Street, Wall Street, https://rockthestreetwallstreet.com/fellas -for-fairness/.

7. Shelley J. Correll, "SWS 2016 Feminist Lecture: Reducing Gender Biases in Modern Workplaces: A Small Wins Approach to Organizational Change," *Gender & Society* 31, no. 6 (2017): 725–50.

8. Jamie Powell, "Hedge Fund Bro Gonna Hedge Fund Bro," *Financial Times*, December 18, 2019, https://ftalphaville.ft.com/2019/12/18/1576674845000 /Hedge-fund-bro-gonna-hedge-fund-bro/.

9. Alison T. Wynn and Shelley J. Correll, "Gendered Perceptions of Cultural and Skill Alignment in Technology Companies," *Social Sciences* 6, no. 2 (2017): 45.

10. Professor Kaplowitz and her students surveyed 430 undergraduate students across eight colleges and universities to evaluate various factors that might encourage women to pursue careers in financial services. They also conducted 12 individual interviews with undergraduate students, of which 75 percent were women and 25 percent were men.

11. Oliver Wyman, *Women in Financial Services 2016* (report), https://www .oliverwyman.com/our-expertise/insights/2016/jun/women-in-financial-services -2016.html.

5. Why Don't Women Choose Investing Careers? The MBA pipeline: Columbia Business School as a Case Study

1. These are data on the class entering in 2019; see https://www8.gsb.columbia .edu/programs/mba/admissions/class-profile.

2. The rankings can be found at http://rankings.ft.com/businessschoolrankings /columbia-business-school/global-mba-ranking-2020#global-mba-ranking -2020.

3. Astrid Jäekel and Tom Moynihan, *Women in Financial Services* (report), Marsh & McLennan Companies, 2016, cited in GAO, *Financial Services Industry: Trends in Management and Representation of Minorities and Women and Diversity Practices, 2007–2015* (report), November 8, 2017, https://www.gao.gov/products/GAO-18-64.

4. Although CBS doesn't release statistics for its faculty, you can get a good sense from its finance faculty directory at https://www8.gsb.columbia.edu /cbs-directory/faculty-search?combine=&field_departments_tid=5575.
5. "Harvard Business School Case Study," *New York Times*, September 8, 2013, https://www.nytimes.com/2013/09/08/education/harvard-case-study-gender -equity.html?.
6. Oliver Wyman, *Women in Financial Services 2016* (report), https://www.oliver -wyman.com/our-expertise/insights/2016/jun/women-in-financial-services -2016.html.

6. Looking Inside Investment Management: Identifying Barriers to Women's Advancement

1. Katty Kay and Claire Shipman, "The Confidence Gap," *Atlantic*, May 2014.
2. Marie Konnikova, "Lean Out: The Dangers for Women Who Negotiate," *New Yorker*, June 10, 2014.
3. Isobel Owen, "Do Women Really Make Better Investors Than Men?," *Financial Times*, April 29, 2019.
4. Cristian L. Dezso, Evan Rawley, and David Gaddis Ross, "The Gender Composition of Firms and Risk-Taking Behavior: Evidence from Mutual Funds," SSRN, August 14, 2018, https://ssrn.com/abstract=3231460 or http://dx.doi.org/10.2139/ssrn.3231460.
5. Malcolm Gladwell, "The Sure Thing," *New Yorker*, January 11, 2010.
6. Thomas Dohmen et al., "Individual Risk Attitudes: Measurement, Determinants, and Behavioral Consequences," *Journal of the European Economic Association* 9, no. 3 (June 2011): 522–50, cited in PwC, *Modern Mobility: Moving Women with Purpose*, 2016, https://www.pwc.com/sg/en/publications/assets /modern-mobility-moving-women-with-purpose.pdf.
7. Stacey Chin, Alexis Krivkovich, and Marie-Claude Nadeau, *Closing the Gap: Leadership Perspectives on Promoting Women in Financial Services*, McKinsey & Company, September 2018.
8. Swethaa Ballakrishnen, Priya Fielding-Singh, and Devon Magliozzi, "Intentional Invisibility: Professional Women and the Navigation of Workplace Constraints," Sociological Perspectives 62, no. 1 (2019), https://journals.sagepub .com/doi/10.1177/0731121418782185.
9. Bill Francis, Thomas Shohfi, and Daqi Xin, "Gender and Earnings Conference Calls" (January 2019), http://www.fmaconferences.org/NewOrleans/Papers /GECC_FMA.pdf.
10. 2019 Stock Market Report from Fidelity Active Investor, January 2, 2020, https://institutional.fidelity.com/app/item/RD_9898021/2019-stock-market -report.html.

11. Gary Stern, "The Scourge of Office Politics in Finance," Institutional Investor, October 23, 2018, https://www.institutionalinvestor.com/article/b1bhxv7oxwfb4c /The-Scourge-of-Office-Politics-in-Finance.

12. Stern, "The Scourge of Office Politics in Finance."

13. Burton G. Malkiel, *A Random Walk Down Wall Street: A Time-Tested Strategy for Successful Investing* (New York: Norton, 2019).

14. In case this might be perceived as an attack, we'll include this postscript on hedge fund performance in a footnote: they have generally delivered returns far behind the S&P 500 and are facing an AUM exodus (sample headline, this one from the *Financial Times*: "Why Some Big Investors Are Tiring of Hedge Funds," January 27, 2020).

15. Catalyst, "Women on Boards: Quick Take," March 13, 2020, https://www .catalyst.org/research/women-on-corporate-boards/.

16. Daniel J. Sandberg, *#Change Pays: There* Were *More Male CEOs Named John, than Female CEOs*, S&P Global Market Intelligence, October 2019, https://www.spglobal.com/marketintelligence/en/documents/changepays _finalwhitepaper.pdf.

17. Reference from Barclays Capital, Hedge Fund Pulse, *Affirmative Investing: Women and Minority Owned Hedge Funds*, June 2011, http://www .managedfunds.org/wp-content/uploads/2011/08/HF-Pulse-Affirmative-Investing -June-2011-Letter.pdf.

18. Leslie Stahl, "Leading by Example to Close the Gender Pay Gap," *60 Minutes*, April 15, 2018, https://www.cbsnews.com/news/salesforce-ceo-marc-benioff -leading-by-example-to-close-the-gender-pay-gap/.

19. Brad M. Barber, Anna Scherbina, and Bernd Schlusche, "Performance Isn't Everything: Personal Characteristics and Career Outcomes of Mutual Fund Managers," SSRN, September 7, 2017 (rev. May 20, 2018), https://papers.ssrn .com/sol3/papers.cfm?abstract_id=3032207.

20. Sreedhari D. Desai, Dolly Chugh, and Arthur P. Brief, "The Implications of Marriage Structure for Men's Workplace Attitudes, Beliefs, and Behaviors Toward Women," *Administrative Science Quarterly* 59, no. 2 (2014): 330–65.

21. Rebecca Fender, ed., *Gender Diversity in Investment Management: New Research for Practitioners on How to Close the Gender Gap* (Charlottesville, VA: CFA Institute Research Foundation, 2016), https://www.cfainstitute.org /-/media/documents/survey/gender-diversity-report.ashx.

22. Barber, Scherbina, and Schlusche, "Performance Isn't Everything."

23. Claire Cain-Miller, "When Wives Earn More than Husbands, Neither Partner Likes to Admit It," *New York Times*, July 17, 2018, https://www .nytimes.com/2018/07/17/upshot/when-wives-earn-more-than-husbands -neither-like-to-admit-it.html.

24. Louise Marie Roth, *Selling Women Short: Gender and Money on Wall Street* (Princeton, NJ: Princeton University Press, 2011).

7. Your Portfolio Is Balanced—Your Life Can Be, Too! Debunking the Work–Life Balance Myth in IM

1. Eve Rodsky, *Fair Play* (New York: Putnam, 2012).
2. Stephanie Koontz, "How to Make Your Marriage Gayer," *New York Times*, February 13, 2020.
3. Natalie Kitroeff and Jessica Silver-Greenberg, "Pregnancy Discrimination Is Rampant Inside America's Biggest Companies," *New York Times*, February 8, 2019.
4. Sandra Lawson, et al., "Closing the Gender Gaps: Advancing Women in Corporate America," Goldman Sachs Global Markets Institute, October 2018, https://www.goldmansachs.com/insights/pages/gmi-gender-gaps.html.
5. Data as of June 30, 2019, https://2020wob.com/.
6. Paul Dolan, *Happy Ever After: Escaping the Myths of a Perfect Life* (London: Allen Lane, 2019).
7. Louise Marie Roth, *Selling Women Short: Gender and Equality on Wall Street* (Princeton, NJ: Princeton University Press, 2015).
8. Matthew Wiswall and Basit Zafar, "Preference for the Workplace, Investment in Human Capital, and Gender," *Quarterly Journal of Economics* 133, no. 1 (2018): 457–507.
9. Renée B. Adams, and Brad M. Barber, and Terrance Odean, "Family, Values, and Women in Finance," SSRN, September 1, 2016, https://ssrn.com/abstract=2827952 or http://dx.doi.org/10.2139/ssrn.2827952.

8. The Constellation: Discussions with Successful Women in Investment Management

1. Stefan Ruenzi, Alexandra Niessen-Ruenzi, and Kristina Meier, "The Impact of Role Models on Women's Self-Selection in Competitive Environments," SSRN, December 14, 2017 (rev. March 25, 2020), https://papers.ssrn.com/sol3/papers.cfm?abstract_id=3087862.
2. Katty Kay and Claire Shipman, "The Confidence Gap," *Atlantic*, May 2014: 1–18, https://www.theatlantic.com/magazine/archive/2014/05/the-confidence-gap/359815/.
3. Daniel Kahneman, *Thinking Fast and Slow* (New York: Farrar, Strauss & Giroux, October 2011).
4. Karim Ansari, "Diversity and Inclusion at the Big 4 Accounting Firms," Undercover Recruiter, accessed November 19, 2020, https://theundercover-recruiter.com/big-4-diversity-and-inclusion/.

10. Solutions—Widening the IM On-Ramp

1. "Bloomberg Marks Launch of New Voices Initiative to Diversify News-room Sources" (press release), April 19, 2018, https://www.bloomberg.com /company/press/bloomberg-marks-launch-of-new-voices-initiative-to-diversify -newsroom-sources/.
2. 100 Women in Finance, "Female Fund Managers," accessed on November 24, 2020, https://100women.org/female-fund-managers/.
3. For more information about GWI, visit http://www.girlswhoinvest.org.
4. For more information about PF, visit http://www.phelpsforward.com.
5. Rebecca Fender, ed., *Gender Diversity in Investment Management: New Research for Practitioners on How to Close the Gender Gap* (Charlottesville, VA: CFA Institute Research Foundation, 2016), https://www.cfainstitute.org /-/media/documents/survey/gender-diversity-report.ashx.
6. UNESCO, *Cracking the Code—Girls' and Women's Education in Science, Technology, Engineering and Mathematics (STEM)* (Paris: UNESCO, 2017), https://unesdoc.unesco.org/ark:/48223/pf0000253479.
7. Max H. Bazerman, Iris Bohnet, and Alexandra Vivien Van Geen, *When Performance Trumps Gender Bias: Joint Versus Separate Evaluation*. Working Paper 12-083 (Boston: Harvard Business School, 2012).
8. Tara Sophia Mohr, "Why Women Don't Apply for Jobs Unless They're 100 Percent Qualified," *Harvard Business Review* (August 25, 2014).
9. Iris Bohnet, *What Works: Gender Equity by Design* (Cambridge, MA: Harvard University Press, 2016).

11. Solutions—Retaining and Promoting Women in IM

1. Zoe Whitton, Edward McKinnon, and Alex Miller, "Men at Work: Where Are We on Work/Life Balance in 2020?," Citi Research, May 2020.
2. Katherine W. Phillips, Katie A. Liljenquist, and Margaret A. Neale, "Is the Pain Worth the Gain? The Advantages and Liabilities of Agreeing with Socially Distinct Newcomers," *Personality and Social Psychology Bulletin* 35, no. 3 (2009): 336–50.
3. K. Zernike, "Gains, and Drawbacks, for Female Professors," *New York Times*, March 21, 2011, https://www.nytimes.com/2011/03/21/us/21mit.html.
4. Iris Bohnet, *What Works: Gender Equity by Design* (Cambridge, MA: Harvard University Press, 2016).
5. McKinsey & Company, *Women in the Workplace 2018*, https://leanin.org /women-in-the-workplace-report-2018/ensure-that-hiring-and-promotions-are -fair.

6. McKinsey & Company, *Women in the Workplace 2018*.

7. CFA Institute, *Gender Diversity in Investment Management*, 2016, https://www.cfainstitute.org/-/media/documents/survey/gender-diversity-report.ashx.

8. Shelley J. Correll and Caroline Simard, "Vague Feedback Is Holding Women Back," *Harvard Business Review*, April 29, 2016, https://hbr.org/2016/04/research-vague-feedback-is-holding-women-back.

9. Linkedin Talent Solutions, *2019 Global Talent Trends*, https://business.linkedin.com/content/dam/me/business/en-us/talent-solutions/resources/pdfs/global_talent_trends_2019_emea.pdf.

10. Max H. Bazerman, Iris Bohnet, and Alexandra Vivien Van Geen, *When Performance Trumps Gender Bias: Joint Versus Separate Evaluation*. Working Paper 12-083 (Boston: Harvard Business School, 2012).

11. Stacey Chin, Alexis Krivkovich, and Marie-Claude Nadeau, *Closing the Gap: Leadership Perspectives on Promoting Women in Financial Services*, McKinsey & Company, September 2018.

12. Lois Joy, "Report: Advancing Women Leaders: The Connection Between Women Board Directors and Women Corporate Officers," Catalyst study, July 15, 2008, https://www.catalyst.org/research/advancing-women-leaders-the-connection-between-women-board-directors-and-women-corporate-officers/.

13. Average of female board representation as of year-end 2019 for the following publicly traded IM firms: Alliance Bernstein, Blackrock, Brookfield, Eaton-Vance, Federated, Franklin, Invesco, Janus, Lazard, and Legg-Mason.

14. Board data sourced from Bloomberg as of the first quarter of 2020 for the following listed IM firms: Franklin, Blackrock, Brookfield, Alliance Bernstein, Eaton Vance, Legg Mason, Federated, Janus, Invesco, and Lazard.

15. Greg Saitz, "Fund Board Diversity, Real and Imagined," *BoardIQ*, May 23, 2017, https://oriongroupltd.com/wp-content/uploads/2018/05/Board-Diversity-study.pdf.

16. Karin Halliday, "Gender Diversity: The Real Reason We Are Still Talking About It," AMP Capital, March 2019, https://www.linkedin.com/pulse/gender-diversity-real-reason-we-still-talking-karin-halliday/.

17. Amy Whyte, "Female Portfolio Managers Made Almost $200K Less Than Male Peers Last Year," *Odyssey Research Partners*, February 12, 2020, https://www.odysseysearchpartners.com/news/female-portfolio-managers-made-almost-200k-less/.

18. A. Hindlian, et al., "Closing the Gender Gaps: Advancing Women in Corporate America," Goldman Sachs Global Markets Institute, October 2018, https://www.goldmansachs.com/insights/pages/gender-pay-gap-f/gmi-gender-gaps.pdf.

19. Jena McGregor, "Citigroup Is Revealing Pay Gap Data Most Companies Don't Want to Share," *Washington Post*, January 16, 2019, https://www.washingtonpost.com/business/2019/01/16/citigroup-is-revealing-pay-gap-data-most-companies-dont-want-share/.

20. Karen Gilchrist, "Citigroup Recorded a 27 Percent Gender Pay Gap—So It Hiked Some Women's Wages," *CNBC*, January 17, 2020, https://www.cnbc .com/2020/01/17/citigroup-reports-27percent-global-gender-pay-gap-announces -rebalancing.html.

21. Federica Cocco, "Would Making Salaries Public Help End Disparities?," *Financial Times*, March 6, 2020, https://www.ft.com/content/7bff2680-4999 -11ea-aee2-9ddbdc86190d.

22. Jeanine Prime and Corrine A. Moss-Racusin, "Engaging Men in Gender Initiatives: What Change Agents Need to Know," Catalyst May 4, 2009, https:// www.catalyst.org/wp-content/uploads/2019/01/Engaging_Men_In_Gender _Initiatives_What_Change_Agents_Need_To_Know.pdf.

23. Gillian Tan and Katia Porzecanski, "Wall Street Rule for the #MeToo Era: Avoid Women at All Cost," Bloomberg, December 3, 2018, https://www .bloomberg.com/news/articles/2018-12-03/a-wall-street-rule-for-the-metoo-era -avoid-women-at-all-cost.

24. Prime and Moss-Racusin, "Engaging Men in Gender Initiatives."

25. Prime and Moss-Racusin, "Engaging Men in Gender Initiatives."

26. Bohnet, *What Works*.

27. Bohnet, *What Works*.

28. Advance Forward at North Dakota State University, *Annual Report Year 7* September 1, 2014–May 31, 2015, https://www.ndsu.edu/fileadmin/forward /reports/NSFADVANCEFORWARDAnnualReport_Year739May2015.pdf.

29. J. Garcia-Alonso et al., "Getting the Most from Your Diversity Dollars," Boston Consulting Group, June 2017, https://www.bcg.com/publications/2017/people -organization-behavior-culture-getting-the-most-from-diversity-dollars.aspx.

30. Frank Dobbin and Alexandra Kalev, "Why Diversity Programs Fail and What Works Better," *Harvard Business Review* 94, nos. 7–8 (2016): 52–60, https://hbr .org/2016/07/why-diversity-programs-fail.

31. Rachel Feintzeig, "Don't Ask Me to Do Office Housework!" *Wall Street* Journal, October 13, 2019, https://www.wsj.com/articles/dont-ask-me-to-do-office -housework-11570959002.

32. Ceri Parker, "It's Official: Women Work Nearly an Hour Longer than Men Every Day," World Economic Forum, June 1, 2017, https://www.weforum .org/agenda/2017/06/its-official-women-work-nearly-an-hour-longer-than -men-every-day/.

33. Dobbin and Kalev, "Why Diversity Programs Fail and What Works Better."

12. Solutions—The Role of Allocators

1. Rajesh Aggarwal and Nicole M. Boyson, "The Performance of Female Hedge Fund Managers," *Review of Financial Economics* 29 (2016): 23–36.

2. 2016 Hedge Fund Rising Stars, https://www.institutionalinvestor.com/article /b14z9mzdq13dg7/the-2016-hedge-fund-rising-stars-samantha-greenberg.

3. Minority- and Women-Owned Business Enterprise, *Asset Management and Financial Institution Strategy Report, 2018–2019 Fiscal Year*, https://osc.state .ny.us/pension/mwbe-report-2018-2019.pdf.

4. Chief Investment Officer, "CalPERS Fires Most of Its Equity Managers," December 4, 2019, https://www.ai-cio.com/news/exclusive-calpers-fires-equity -managers/.

5. New York State Division of Minority and Women's Business Development, "MWBE Certification Frequently Asked Questions," https://cdn.esd.ny.gov /MWBE/Data/FAQ_flyer_FINAL.pdf. A firm is allowed "to be certified as a MWBE in their home state, if a similar process exists, and be registered and authorized to conduct business in the state of New York and have a presence in the New York State."

6. CFA Institute, *Global Investment Performance Standards for Firms— 2020*, https://www.cfainstitute.org/-/media/documents/code/gips/2020-gips -standards-firms.ashx?Campaign%20Lead%20=utm_source%3DSMO &s_cid=smo_CFA20A_FB_SA_GIPSstandards.

7. Josh Lerner and Bella Research Group, *Diversifying Investments: A Study of Ownership Diversity in the Asset Management Industry*, Knight Foundation, January 29, 2019, https://knightfoundation.org/reports/diversifying-investments -a-study-of-ownership-diversity-and-performance-in-the-asset-management -industry/

8. J. Lerner et al., *2018 Diverse Asset Management Firm Assessment, Final Report, January 2019*, https://www.sec.gov/files/amac-background-2018-diverse -asset-management.pdf.

9. Barclays Capital, *Affirmative Investing: Women and Minority Owned Hedge Funds*, June 2011, https://2rp8zq2kdoxy38kvwx23zbuc-wpengine .netdna-ssl.com/wp-content/uploads/2020/04/research-affirmative-investing .pdf.

10. Thurman T. White, Jr., *Who Manages the Money? A Case Study of the W. R. Kellogg Foundation*, ABFE, September 2014, https://www.abfe.org/wp-content /uploads/2014/10/White+Paper+-+Who+Manages+the+Money+14.pdf.

11. White, *Who Manages the Money?*

12. NAIC, *Examining the Returns. The Financial Returns of Diverse Private Equity Firms*, 2017, https://naicpe.com/examining-the-results-the-financial -returns-of-diverse-private-equity-firms/.

13. The Verizon case study was referred to in Barclays Capital, *Affirmative Investing: Women and Minority Owned Hedge Funds*.

14. Barclays Capital, *Affirmative Investing: Women and Minority Owned Hedge Funds*.

15. J. Loren, "Princeton Looks to Break Up the White Male Money Monopoly," May 9, 2019, https://www.bloomberg.com/news/features/2019-05-09/princeton-looks-to-break-up-the-white-male-money-monopoly.
16. See https://www.billiejeanking.com/equality/title-ix/.
17. From Generation Investment Management's website, https://www.generationim.com/firm-overview/our-people/.
18. Loren, "Princeton Looks to Break Up the White Male Money Monopoly."
19. NAIC, *Examining the Returns*.
20. Rachel Levy, "Hedge-Fund Giant Citadel Hires Manager Away from Her Own Fund," *Wall Street Journal*, February 19, 2019, https://www.wsj.com/articles/hedge-fund-giant-citadel-hires-manager-away-from-her-own-fund-11550595309.
21. L. J. Brock and J. Pinchfield, "Why We Modeled Our Hiring Process on the NFL and NASA," *Harvard Business Review*, January 25, 2018, https://hbr.org/2018/01/why-we-modeled-our-hiring-process-on-the-nfl-and-nasa.
22. E. Carson and M. Miller, *Investment Manager Diversity. The Hardest Taboo to Break*, February 2014, https://www.siliconvalleycf.org/sites/default/files/publications/investment-manager-diversity-hardest-taboo-to-break-casestudy.pdf.

Glossary

ACTIVE INVESTING Compared with passive investing, defined below; the portfolio manager managing the pool of investments has discretion to choose what the PM considers to be the best investments in accordance with the limitations in the fund's prospectus.

ALTERNATIVES An alternative investment is a type of investment that does not fall into one of the conventional categories of equity, fixed income, or cash. It includes private equity, venture capital, hedge funds, real estate, and other types of nonconventional investments.

ASSETS UNDER MANAGEMENT (AUM) This is the total market value of the investments that a person, entity, or firm manages on behalf of their clients.

BUY SIDE The buy side refers to a diverse range of investment firms, from pension funds to mutual funds to endowments. The firms are investing money. The term is used often in contrast to analysts: buy-side analysts work for investment firms and consume the research product of sell-side analysts who work for investment banks.

CAREER ANALYST This is an analyst who does not want to become a portfolio manager but, rather, chooses to work as an analyst throughout her career.

CLIENT PORTFOLIO MANAGER (ALSO KNOWN AS AN INSTITUTIONAL PORT-FOLIO MANAGER) Although this term sounds similar to the PM title, people in this role are not responsible for investing a fund's assets. These are a fund's investor relations people, who explain its strategy, performance, and stock selection process to potential and current investors.

DEFINED BENEFIT PLAN (DB PLAN) This is a type of retirement plan in which the employer makes contributions. It pays out a predetermined amount on an employee's retirement (usually a percentage of final salary) that is not linked to the returns of the underlying assets in the plan.

DEFINED CONTRIBUTION PLAN (DC PLAN) A DC plan is a type of retirement plan in which the employer and the employee make contributions. These funds are then invested according to the preferences of the employee and based on the returns of those underlying assets. On the employee's retirement, there will be a pool of moneys that have accumulated tax free and can be withdrawn as needed.

ENDOWMENT This is a nonprofit organization that has been endowed with money or property and uses the resulting investment income for a specific purpose.

ERISA ERISA is the acronym for the Employee Retirement Income Security Act of 1974. It is a federal law that sets minimum standards for most voluntarily established pension and health plans in private industry to provide protection for the individuals who have a claim on the assets in these plans (the plan participants). ERISA requires the fiduciaries of the plan assets to be accountable to the participants for the decisions that they make regarding the investment and management of the fund's assets.

ESG OR IMPACT INVESTING ESG stands for environmental, social, and governance. This style of investment management involves investment in companies that are considered to have superior ESG performance compared with other investment opportunities. This umbrella term describes a variety of investment approaches that invest in companies based on their pursuing positive social, environmental, or governance actions.

EXCHANGE-TRADED FUND (ETF) An exchange-traded fund is a basket of securities that tracks an underlying index. It can include a variety of types of investments, including bonds, equities, and commodities.

FAMILY OFFICE This refers to a private wealth management firm that handles the financial capital of wealthy individuals and/or families. These firms often provide clients with other services, such as household staff management, travel arrangements, estate planning, and tax and accounting matters.

FINANCIAL ADVISOR (FA) This person provides financial services or guidance to clients, for example, by constructing portfolios of stock and bond mutual funds.

FOUNDATIONS Similar to endowments, foundations usually manage a pool of money that is donated by many individuals to provide support for a particular cause or entity.

INDEXING This is a style of investment management whereby the investment performance is designed to mimic the performance of an underlying index, such as the S&P 500 or the Dow Jones. This is another term for "passive investing."

INSTITUTIONAL INVESTOR The term describes a company or organization that invests money on behalf of clients or members, such as a pension, endowment, or foundation.

INVESTMENT MANAGEMENT (IM) This is a process whereby an organization is responsible for the buying and selling of investments on behalf of an individual or an institution. It most often refers to managing the holdings within an investment portfolio, often a mutual fund.

MINORITY- AND WOMEN-OWNED BUSINESS ENTERPRISE (MWBE) An MWBE is a for-profit business that is at least 51 percent owned, operated, capitalized, and controlled by members who are identified as being minorities and/or women.

MUTUAL FUND This is an investment vehicle made up of a pool of money collected from many investors and managed by professional investors. These managers can invest in equities, fixed income, commodities, and other types of securities depending on the limitations in the mutual fund's prospectus.

PASSIVE INVESTING This strategy of investing seeks to replicate the returns of a referenced index (e.g., the S&P 500). Index investing is considered a form of passive investing. Passive investing is considered the opposite of active investing.

PENSION PLAN Such a plan is a retirement vehicle to which employers contribute money to be invested to provide benefits for employees once they retire.

PORTFOLIO MANAGER (PM) This person is responsible for investing a mutual, exchange-traded, or closed-end fund's assets, or those of an individual or an institutional investor.

QUALIFIED INSTITUTIONAL BUYER (QIB) A QIB is a purchaser of securities who is deemed by U.S. law to be financially sophisticated and is legally recognized by securities market regulators as needing less protection from issuers compared with most public investors.

SELL SIDE This term is used in the financial services to refer to firms that sell investment services to investment management firms (the buy side).

SHORTING Shorting involves selling shares of stocks that you do not currently own. It is typically executed based on the premise that the shares will decline in value and can be acquired at a later date at a cheaper price.

SOCIAL PILLAR SCORE This score reflects a company's performance regarding workforce, human rights, community, and product responsibility as well as corporate governance metrics such as management and shareholder and corporate social responsibility measures.

TICKER SYMBOL A ticker symbol is an arrangement of characters—usually letters—that represent a particular security listed on an exchange or otherwise traded publicly. The ticker symbol does not need to be the shortened version of the name of the company. For example, the ticker symbol for Franklin Resources, Inc., the firm where one of your authors works, is BEN (for Benjamin Franklin).

TRANSACTION COSTS In the context of investment management, these are the costs incurred when buying and selling securities, including broker commissions and bid-ask spreads.

Index

Page numbers in *italics* indicate figures or tables.

Index

Wall Street, gender diversity on, 56
Wall Street (film), 61
The Wall Street Journal, 123
Wasserman, Melanie, 41
wealth gap, 165
"Where Are All the Women?" (*Institutional Investor*), 97
white men, 61, 184, 185
White Men as Full Diversity Partners (WMFDP), 184
WIN. *See* Women in Investing
W.K. Kellogg study, 201, 202
WMFDP. *See* White Men as Full Diversity Partners
Wolfe, Lauren Taylor, 121, 130
The Wolf of Wall Street (film), 54, 61, 92, 216
"Wolf of Wall Street" myth, 54
women, ix, x, xii, 155; advocates for, 214–15; barriers for, 80, 87–88, 117; biases against, 43, 166; in boardroom, 179–80, 238n13; in classrooms, 67, 81–83; confidence and, 90–91; discrimination against, 33, 171–72, 178; exposure to, 63–64, 66–67, 69; as investment analysts, 23–24; Latina, 65; math skills and, 62; in medicine, 40–42; men commenting on, 94; as PMs,

18, 23–24, 154; quotes about, 42; recruitment of, 69, 157–58; representation in finance of, 36; single, 113; wage gap regression for men *versus*, 109
Women in Investing (WIN) conference, 84, 162–63, 225
women on boards study, 49
"women-owned firm," 199
workaholics, 116
work cycle, 119
work environment, 27
workforce balance, 213–14
work-from-home transition, COVID-19, 108
work hours, flexible, 40–41, 107, 115–16, 149
working, remote-, 115, 116
working mothers, 108–9, 147–48; prototype 1 for, 110–11; prototype 2 for, 111–12; prototype 3 for, 112; prototype 4 for, 113–14
working women, negativity toward, 103–4
work–life balance, 52, 106–7, 125
workplace gender dynamics, 87
work–work balance, 147
writing: concise, 145–46; novels, 143
wrong, being, 89–90

259

CPSIA information can be obtained
at www.ICGtesting.com
Printed in the USA
BVHW072303080223
658150BV00006B/13/J